MW00575478

Rock Lick Method
for Guitar

Master the Licks, Techniques and Concepts
You Need to Become an
Awesome Rock and Metal Guitarist

by James Shipway

Rock Lick Method for Guitar
by James Shipway

Published by Headstock Books
headstockbooks.com

Copyright © James Shipway 2023

All rights reserved. This book or parts thereof may not be reproduced in any form, stored in any retrieval system, or transmitted in any form by any means - electronic, mechanical, photocopy, recording, or otherwise - without prior written permission of the publisher, except as provided by the United Kingdom copyright law. For permission requests, contact: info@headstockbooks.com

Paperback ISBN: 978-1-914453-16-8
Hardcover ISBN: 978-1-914453-17-5 / 978-1-914453-18-2
Ebook ISBN: 978-1-914453-15-1

Search for 'james shipway guitar' on YouTube and
subscribe for hours of free video lessons!

Join my online community at **totalguitarlab.com** and
get instant access to *all* my premium guitar courses *plus* live training,
workshops and Q&A sessions.

Contents

Get Your Free Download Pack
Before You Begin!

This book comes with free downloadable bonus content including:

- **Demonstration videos** showing you the licks and concepts found in this book
- **Backing tracks** for you to practice the licks over
- Your **Blank tab practice workbook** to use for recording your own licks and ideas (you'll discover a lot of these as you work through this book)

How To Get Your Bonus Content

To get your download pack you'll need to go to this webpage and follow the instructions:

headstockbooks.com/rock

Sometimes people have difficulty reaching the download pages. This is normally easily fixed. If you have problems accessing the webpage then:

- Check that you have typed in the **exact web address** given, simply going to the website will not take you to the correct page!
- **Clear your browser cache** and try again. This often fixes the problem
- Try a **different browser** or device
- If all else fails, go to **headstockbooks.com** and head for the **downloads page** in the menu. Locate the image of this book and click on it to be taken to the correct page

If you've done all these things and *still* can't get to the page then email us at **info@headstockbooks.com** for help.

The web address for your free downloads again is:

headstockbooks.com/rock

Introduction

Welcome to the **Rock Lick Method for Guitar** book, it's great to have you here!

The purpose of this book is to teach you most of what you need to know to play authentic, awesome sounding rock and metal guitar solos. Within these easy-to-follow lessons you're going to discover:

- The most important playing techniques you need to know
- The 'must-know' scales and theory used by rock guitarists *most* of the time
- Essential rock licks used by all the rock guitar legends
- Complete solos demonstrating how to put it all together
- How to build your very own vocabulary of soloing ideas for developing a rock guitar style which is uniquely yours
- Plus, how to build playing speed, creating guitar solos of your own, tips for getting a great rock guitar sound ...and much more!

As with all my books, the overall aim is to go *beyond* just showing you things to play on the guitar. Instead, I hope to give you what you need to get in touch with your musical imagination so that you can eventually conceive and express creative musical ideas of your *own*. This is what all the greatest guitar players have been able to do. If this sounds too difficult for where you're at right now, don't worry - once you begin using some of the concepts and exercises I'm going to give you in this book, you'll soon see your musical creativity begin to break through. Just trust the process laid out in this book, do the work, and I'm pretty certain you'll be surprised by what you can achieve.

Who Is This Book For?

The lessons in this book assume you already possess some knowledge and technical skill when it comes to playing rock guitar, but no matter what your level of expertise, you can derive enormous benefit from what I'm going to teach you.

If you're an intermediate level guitar player who already has some experience of playing rock solos and licks, then you're *perfectly* suited to this book. The ideas I'm going to share will build on what you already know.

But don't be put off if you're brand new to rock soloing - you can still use this book. Some of the techniques, concepts and examples I present may take a while to get the hang of - but you'll be learning the essentials of great rock playing much more thoroughly than most beginners do. This should help you to avoid the common mistakes, false starts and roadblocks most beginners inevitably experience. If you're prepared to be patient, and when necessary to simplify things a bit, then you'll likely build the core, foundational knowledge you need to play rock guitar much faster and more easily than most players.

For the advanced player, this book will provide you with an easy way to refresh your knowledge and skills, build your soloing vocabulary, and scale new heights in your musical imagination.

How To Use This Book (for best results)

To get the most out of this book consider the following practical guidelines:

- Don't neglect Chapter 1: *Essential Knowledge All Rock Guitarists Need*. This chapter is there to ensure you have the required knowledge to work successfully through the remainder of the book. You may already know some of what is covered but go through the entire chapter anyway - it's important!
- Go slowly through the lessons. It's always tempting to hurry the learning process, but in my experience it never pays off. Go at a sensible pace and *enjoy* the journey
- Find ways to *use* new material as soon as you can. For example, write a solo which uses a new lick you've learned, practice using a new scale shape over a jamtrack, try out new ideas and techniques at band practice etc. I'll be giving you exercises throughout to help you do this
- Working through the lessons in order is probably the best plan of action. If you're already an experienced and fluent rock player then you may want to study the material in a different way, but you may need to backtrack a little if I refer to something you missed earlier
- Periodically record yourself playing certain licks/exercises from this book so you can self-critique your playing and progress. This is a great way to spot areas where you need to improve
- Listen out for your favourite players using the licks, techniques and concepts this book teaches you - they almost certainly are!
- Don't put too much pressure on yourself to improve. I used to be guilty of this, and it took much of the enjoyment out of playing the guitar. Practice as often as possible and take your practice sessions seriously, but make sure that the process is inspiring, rewarding and fun

Adapt these guidelines a little to suit you if you wish, but try to adhere to the general principle of each one - they can make a big difference to how much benefit and fun you get from this book.

About the Examples in this Book

The examples in this book will give you loads of ideas which you can use in your guitar solos. When writing these examples:

- I've chosen to steer clear of super-specialised concepts and techniques, and tried to give you versatile licks and ideas which you can actually *use* in a musical setting

- I've opted to give you examples which most players will be able to play with a bit of practice. The examples will probably challenge you, but there are no 'impossible-shred licks', these are not what this book is about
- I've presented examples similar to core ideas heard in the styles of pretty much *all* rock and metal players to help you become an authentic sounding rock soloist

It's impossible to make all examples the perfect level of difficulty for *every* reader of this book, so if you find an example is too hard, then simplify it to make it possible for you to play right now. This will get you started with it whilst you gradually work up to playing the more challenging version. Don't make things *too* easy, working on things we can't yet do is how we improve - but struggling with something *way* beyond your level of ability isn't normally that productive.

Some readers may find some of the examples *too* easy. If so, find ways to make them more challenging - play them faster, add stretches etc. The idea is to find a way to make everything in this book *work for you*, whilst still pushing yourself so that you expand your capabilities on the guitar.

What Is Not Covered

I'm not even going to try to cover 60+ years of rock guitar development in a single book. My aim is not to teach you *everything*, my aim is to present *most* of what you need to play authentic rock solos.

This book focuses on the rock guitar style which has emerged since the late 1960's. It started with players like Jimi Hendrix, Jimmy Page and Eric Clapton before being picked up and developed later by guitarists like Michael Schenker, Angus Young, Gary Moore, Tony Iommi, Randy Rhoads, Ritchie Blackmore, Edward Van Halen, Slash - as well as literally *thousands* of other great players. Whilst all these guitarists are unique, there is a *core* rock guitar vocabulary which they all share, and which makes up a big part of their playing styles. Learning, executing, and developing this core vocabulary is what we will be focusing on in this book.

There are many rock guitar topics I will *not* be addressing in this book. Things like two-handed tapping, sweep-picking, whammy bar tricks, neo-classical styles and advanced harmonic techniques are not covered. It's not that these things aren't interesting or useful, they're just not *essential* in order to play convincing rock guitar. In my experience, if someone can't yet do what this book teaches, they'll struggle to make these things work anyway. There are *many* resources available if you ever want to explore areas like tapping or sweep picking, so look around and see what you can find.

Music Theory Knowledge

You definitely *don't* need to be a music theory expert to use this book, but basic knowledge of music theory will definitely be a help. In these lessons I do mention things like:

- Major and minor keys
- Major and minor pentatonics
- Basic intervals (octave, b3rd, b7th, b5th etc)

- Relative major and relative minor

Some of these theory topics are explained a little, but I don't go into great depth on them - it's not the purpose of this book.

If you *haven't* got a basic understanding of music theory, then check out my 3 book series, **Music Theory for Guitarists**. The first volume will quickly teach you the theory basics you need to easily understand everything in this book. If you want to know more, then Volumes 2 and 3 take your theory to almost pro-level. This popular series is easy to read and follow, and is well worth grabbing. You can get each volume separately, or get the complete collection in a single edition.

Rhythm Reading

It is **not** essential to be able to read music or rhythm to use this book, but basic rhythm reading skills will certainly be helpful. I'll also be using rhythmic language like *quarter notes*, *16th notes*, *triplets* and *sextuplets* - so understanding these terms will also be a help.

Rather than clog up the main body of this book with rhythm reading lessons, I've created **Appendix 2: Rhythm Reading Basics**. This is at the back of this book and designed to give you a quick crash-course in a few essentials. I recommend you work through this information, it will help you learn, understand, and use the content of this book - plus, basic rhythm reading skills are useful for any musician.

Guitar Gear

Getting an authentic rock guitar sound is an important part of becoming a good rock player. You may already know what you need to know on this topic and have a sound you're happy with, but if you need a few tips on guitars, strings, amps and other equipment then see **Appendix 1: Rock Guitar Gear**.

How This Book Is Structured

The material in this book is presented in a few different ways. I've done this to break it up and make it more manageable without leaving out anything important.

Chapters focus on specific topics, for example blues/rock power licks, major pentatonic soloing, or sliding licks and runs.

Quickfire Lessons are dotted throughout the chapters. These summarise important topics and techniques, telling you most of what you need to know without it taking pages and pages.

Solo Studies are introduced at various points in the book. These aim to give you a 'real life' example of how you might use certain ideas in the context of a complete guitar solo.

Most of the example licks feature a **Lick Challenge** shown underneath the tablature. These are included to get you experimenting with the licks and ideas I show you. The process of experimentation and discovery will help you find new licks and ideas of your own which you can employ in your solos. This is an important part of the learning journey and will help you become a more creative musician - so don't neglect this extra step when you learn a new lick.

By presenting everything in this way, I hope to make this book easier and more enjoyable to use. This will mean that more guitar players can benefit from and have more fun with everything it contains.

About the Backing Tracks and Videos

As mentioned earlier, I've supplied you with **video demonstrations** of the majority of examples in this book. These give you the chance to see them played up close and hear them demonstrated at a few different speeds. In the videos, examples are demonstrated over one of the **backing tracks** I've also supplied you with. Of course, feel free to practice them along to different backing tracks as well.

I've given you **backing tracks** for all the **solo studies** in this book. This gives you the opportunity to practice them along with the backing track on your own. These backing tracks are named according to whichever solo study they go along with.

You also get a variety of **backing tracks** for use with **lick examples and exercises**. These cover all the keys used for the examples in this book as well as giving you some various tempos/grooves to choose from. If you want to practice a lick in this book over a backing track use one of the tracks in the same key as the example you wish to practice. You'll also need to use the track which uses a tempo at which you can play the example. Don't forget to search out other backing tracks to use too, there are millions available for free on platforms like YouTube. Doing this will help you get used to using the material in this book in all sorts of different musical settings.

To get your free **downloadable bonus pack** containing the videos, backing tracks, plus a few more goodies - see the **start of this book**.

That's It For Now...

Ok, I think we're ready to get started. I'm really excited about what this book is going to help you to achieve, and I hope you are too.

So grab your guitar and dive straight into Chapter 1: *Essentials You Need For Great Rock Guitar*.

Good luck!

Chapter 1:
Essentials You Need For Great Rock Guitar

Before we dive into the main body of this book there are some important introductory topics we need to discuss - this is the purpose of this chapter. We're going to cover:

- The most important scales you need to play rock guitar
- Important technique tips you need to be aware of (and mistakes to avoid)

Failing to understand some of this material could easily hold you up, so it makes sense to cover it right at the start. You will probably know at least some of this information already, but study it carefully anyway - it really is important.

Common Rock Scales

Scales are the tools we use to play licks and solos. This book mainly focuses on the most common scales employed by rock guitarists - the **minor pentatonic** and **blues scale**. These scales have come to define the sound of rock guitar. Let's look at how to play these, just in case you haven't seen them before.

The Minor Pentatonic Scale

The following fretboard diagram shows the most common pattern used to play the minor pentatonic scale. This is often called the 'shape 1' minor pentatonic pattern, and this is how I'll refer to it in this book. It is shown in the key of A minor (more on keys in a moment).

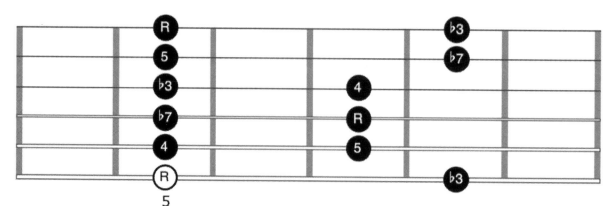

You can see that the notes in the scale are numbered - these are the *intervals* that make up the scale. If you're not sure what this means then don't worry, you can still use this book. Knowing about intervals is very helpful though so see my **Music Theory for Guitarists** series to learn the simple theory behind them.

Also notice how the note on the low E string is shown in white and labelled 'R'. This is the **root** note and knowing how to use it is very important. Let's quickly look at this before we move on.

The Root Note and Moving the Scale Pattern

The 'shape 1' scale pattern can be moved to different locations on the fretboard and used to play the minor pentatonic scale in *any* key. Whichever note the root becomes when we move the pattern, tells us which minor pentatonic scale we are playing. The following diagram shows the notes along the low E string:

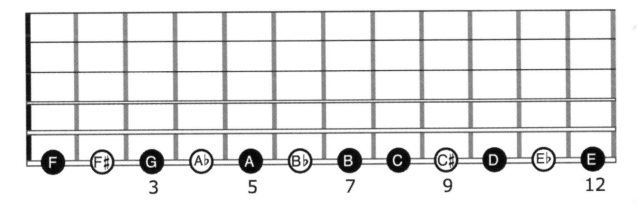

You can begin the pattern on *any* of these notes to get whichever minor pentatonic scale you need. If we started the pattern on G (3rd fret) we'd get G minor pentatonic. Start on E (12th fret) and we get E minor pentatonic.

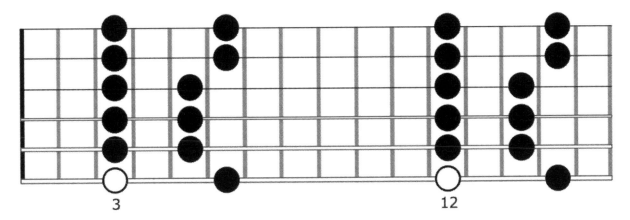

Understanding this system enables you to use *one* scale pattern to play in *all* keys. Spend some time getting comfortable with this system, it's *really* important - then test yourself with the tasks that follow.

Use the root note in the pattern to play the following minor pentatonic scales:

1.   C minor pentatonic
2.   D minor pentatonic
3.   F minor pentatonic
4.   C# minor pentatonic
5.   B*b* minor pentatonic

The Blues Scale

We can decorate the minor pentatonic scale by adding the *b*5th (*'flattened fifth'*) interval to the other notes. This gives the scale a slightly darker flavour which, in most rock players opinions, sounds great. This 'decorated' minor pentatonic scale is normally referred to as the *blues scale*. The following diagram shows you how to play the 'shape 1' blues scale in the key of A. Notice how it is simply the minor pentatonic scale with the added *b*5th note (shown as a black square).

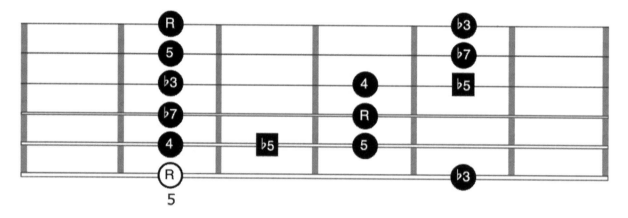

Of course, the *b*5th note can be added to the minor pentatonic scale in any key. The following image shows the G and E minor pentatonic patterns from a moment ago adapted to become the G and E blues scales.

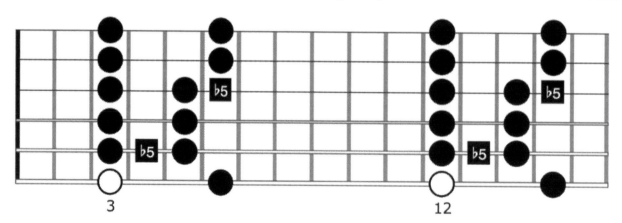

It's good to understand the difference between these two scales, but ultimately you can kind of think of them as being the same thing. When we play we tend to use them interchangeably - so you don't need to think of them as two distinct scales with distinct applications. This makes them easier to remember and use as well.

Later on in this book we'll examine some other scales - but the shape 1 minor pentatonic and blues scales are the only scale patterns you need to use chapters 1-4. Make sure to get as familiar with these patterns - we're going to be using them a lot.

I don't want to distract you from this book, but if you ever want to learn more about the minor pentatonic scale and how to use it then you might want to see my book, **CAGED System for Guitar**. In that book you'll learn all 5 minor pentatonic scale shapes so you can learn to solo with the scale *anywhere* on the fretboard. It also features sample licks from each pattern to help you learn to use it effectively. This could be a valuable resource for you sometime in the future.

Technique Essentials and Tips

This book is not specifically about guitar technique, but developing good playing technique is important if you want to become a fluent player who is able to execute their musical ideas effectively. We'll be discussing important playing techniques and topics throughout this book, but let's look at some technique essentials before you get started. This will help you make good progress right out of the gate.

Fretting Hand Fingers

How our fretting hand fingers perform has a big impact on our playing, so we want to train them to operate as efficiently as possible. To achieve this, consider the following guidelines.

- In general, keep your fingers as close to the strings as possible. Try to stop them 'flying away' from the fretboard as you play
- Try to eliminate any unnecessary movement in your fingers
- Keep them relaxed and loose

Many of the examples in this book feature my recommended fingering, shown by the small numbers above the notes in the tab. I've given you what I think is the best fingering option in *most* situations. I say *most* situations because there isn't really a 'best way' to play something, it depends on what you're playing before and after it. Following the fingerings given will help you develop good methods for playing common rock phrases, but you may find alternative methods which work better for you.

There are some hotly debated topics when it comes to fingering. My take on these is based on my experience as both a player and teacher, but be warned: you're sure to encounter people who disagree with my opinion! Let's take a quick look at some of these now.

Thumb: behind or over the neck?

Some people are *adamant* that your thumb should stay behind the neck at *all* times, but this is not something many of the best players seem to do. I think the best place for your thumb depends on *what you're playing*. If I'm performing a stretch my thumb tends to move behind the neck. If I'm performing a string bend or vibrato my thumb goes over the top of the neck. I suggest being flexible instead of following a 'rule'.

Should you use 'one finger per fret'?

No! The 'one finger per fret' approach can work sometimes, but you definitely *don't* want to be bound by it. I think we should always use the easiest, most effective way to play something instead of dogmatically following a 'system'.

Should you always use your pinky/4th finger?

Many classic rock licks are best played with only the first three fingers on your fretting hand. Don't *neglect* your pinky finger, you need to be able to use it - but don't use it just for the sake of it. The fingerings for the examples will guide you as to when you might use the 4th finger and when you might not.

Should your fingers fret the strings on their fingertips?

There are exceptions, but in general, keep your fingers *slightly flat* rather than right on the fingertips. This is part of developing good muting technique (more on this next).

Muting and Damping Technique

Controlling the string noise that a distorted electric guitar produces is essential, and this is where muting or damping technique comes in. The basic idea is to silence the strings you are *not* playing by gently touching them, stopping them from ringing out. Both the fretting and picking hands have a role to play.

Picking Hand Muting

Using the picking hand to mute with is sometimes called **palm muting**. Basically, part of the picking hand acts as a 'muffler', gently resting on the strings to keep them quiet. With a little experimentation you'll find this soon feels quite natural. A few guidelines:

- Exactly where you mute and which part of your hand you use will depend on your picking position. Experiment till you find a way that works for you
- Don't *press down* on the strings - just rest **very lightly** on them, a soft touch is all you need
- Muting is one reason why your picking hand should stay close to the strings. It should actually be resting *on* the strings much of the time

Video 1.1 shows my picking hand and muting position. You don't have to copy me exactly, but you should be able to see the above principles at work.

Many players avoid muting because they're worried about muting the strings they *want* to hear. Consequently they never learn to perform this crucial technique. The key is trial and error, if you persevere you'll quickly find your palm muting begins to come together.

Picking hand muting is generally used on the strings which are lower (in pitch) than the string you are playing. This is because your hand can't really mute the strings on the *other* side of the pick, and this is where the fretting hand comes to the rescue.

Fretting Hand Muting

The general idea is that the fretting hand fingers lightly touch any unused strings to mute them. This sounds complicated, but with a suitable finger position you'll often find you naturally do it. A few guidelines to help are:

- In general, keep your fingers close to the strings. Fingers which are a long way from the strings will not be able to mute
- Keep your fingers *slightly flat* rather than on the fingertips. When you play a note, the tip and the fingerprint part of your finger can lightly touch the adjacent strings to help silence them
- Unused fingers can lie gently on the strings behind the finger we're using (almost like a capo)
- When you fret a note, get used to 'stubbing-up' against the neighbouring string with your fingertip
- There should not be a gap between the neighbouring string and the tip of the finger. See this demonstrated in the video

You can see some of these things happening in **video 1.1**.

Be patient as you develop your fretting hand muting, it normally takes longer to grasp than palm muting does.

By muting with *both* hands you can develop a bullet-proof muting technique which will keep unwanted string noise to a minimum. Don't feel like you need *perfect* muting technique *before* you play anything, you can develop it as you go. If you monitor your playing for unwanted noise, then tweak your technique to rectify it, your muting technique will naturally improve over time. Sure, string noise can be annoying, but don't get frustrated - just do what you need to fix it.

Hammer-Ons and Pull-Offs

Fretting hand techniques like hammer-ons, pull-offs and slides are used extensively by rock players, and are in most of the examples in this book. I'm going to assume you know what hammer-ons and pull-offs are, but let's look at some general tips for executing them well.

Hammer-Ons

When performing a hammer-on:

- Hammer-on firmly and decisively. Hammering on too slowly will give you an inferior sound
- Executing the hammer-on with *too much* of the 'fingerprint' part of your finger tends to produce noise and unclear notes. Hammer-on with a good amount of fingertip. You don't need to be *right* on the tips, but your fingers don't want to be *too* flat.
- Use as little movement as needed in order to generate a sharp, clean note. As with other techniques, unnecessary movement slows us down and makes things harder
- In general, as you hammer-on, avoid letting the other fingers lift up/come away from the fretboard. In general keep them as close to the strings as possible

Try applying these tips to some simple exercises. There are thousands of possibilities, but hammering-on up and down a minor pentatonic scale is a good option. Picking indications (more on these shortly) and fingering are shown above the tab. I suggest you *also* play the entire exercise using *only* your **1st and 3rd** fingers to get used to stretching with your fretting hand.

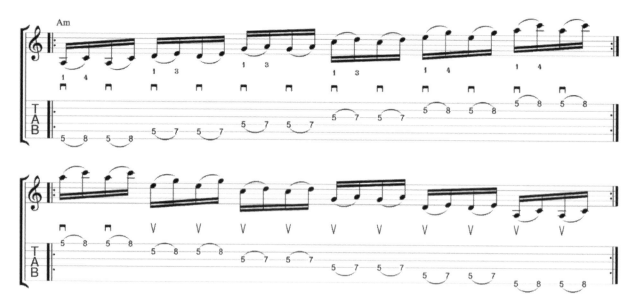

Pull-Offs

When executing a pull-off:

- Pull your finger slightly *downwards* instead of just lifting it up. It will 'flick' the string producing a clear note
- You do need *some* tension in your finger to execute the pull-off, but don't use too much. The pull-off should still feel like a small, relaxed movement
- Avoid unnecessary movement as you pull-off - aim for a small 'flick'
- In general, avoid letting the other fingers come away from the fretboard - keep them as close to the strings as possible
- Make sure the finger you are pulling-off to is in place in time. The 'flick' generated by the pull-off will sound this note for you, but not if it is not being fretted!

Apply these principles to the following pentatonic pull-off exercise. Picking and fingering indications are shown above the tab. As with the hammer-on exercise, I recommend you *also* play this using *only* your **1st and 3rd** fingers - this will cultivate the super-important stretch between them (we'll be using this a lot).

The term **legato** is often used to describe the smooth, flowing sound created by using techniques like hammer-ons and pull-offs. Some players base their guitar style around the legato sound and techniques, picking as few notes as possible - other players prefer the sound they get with more picked notes.

It really depends how you want to sound, but most players use at least some legato techniques in their playing. Following these tips will help bring your legato techniques up to scratch no matter how you choose to use them.

Picking Techniques

Trying to describe the 'best' way to use the pick is impossible, picking techniques vary a lot from player to player. There are however a few things which most good pickers have in common, so consider the following when it comes to your picking technique:

- How you hold the pick is a personal thing, so experiment. Most players hold it between the thumb and 1st finger but some players prefer to use 3 fingers instead. Use what feels natural for you
- Too much pick protruding from your hand is generally harder to use - try to use as little of the pick as you can
- Keep your hand and the pick near the strings (for muting!)
- The picking hand and fingers need to stay relaxed, too much tension will hinder your picking and affect the sound of your notes
- In general, make your pick strokes as small as possible. Excess movement slows you down and makes it harder to be accurate with the pick

Check out some videos of players like Paul Gilbert, Steve Morse, John Petrucci and Zakk Wylde. All these players are awesome pickers, but their technique is quite different. They might give you some ideas about how you want your picking style to develop.

I mostly use an **alternate picking** technique. This is where we generally alternate between up and down strokes with the pick. Whilst not perfect, after years of experimentation, I've found this works best for me most of the time.

Some players prefer **economy picking**. This method does not use strict alternating down and up pick strokes. When moving from a low string to a high string we use a down pick. When moving from a high string to a low string we use an up pick. This can make crossing strings easier.

The following example illustrates the same phrase played using these two picking methods. Picking indications are shown above the TAB. The symbol for an up pick is '**V**'. The other symbol which looks like an '**incomplete box**' is the symbol for a down pick. Check out the example so that you understand the differences between the two approaches.

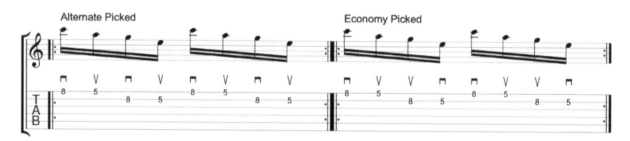

So which is best? In my opinion, neither - they both have advantages and disadvantages. I've tried out both methods extensively during my playing career, and have concluded that alternate picking is what works best for *me* most of the time. I find my rhythmic feel and phrasing is better. On the other hand, the logic of the economy picking approach is hard to argue against. You need to go with whichever method works for *you*, and it may take a bit of trial and error to decide which you prefer - some players use both ways depending on what they're playing.

The examples in this book show how *I* would pick them, and the picking shown is a recommendation only - feel free to change it to suit the picking approach you like to use.

String Bending

The importance of mastering bending cannot be overstated, and nothing spoils the sound of someone's playing like the sound of sloppy, out of tune bends! This is why we're looking at this crucial guitar technique right at the start of this book.

You will see players who bend differently from how I'm describing here - but I'm convinced this is the best way, giving you the control and strength needed to get your bends sounding awesome. Feel free to disagree and do it differently, although personally I don't recommend it!

What is string bending?

In simple terms, string bending is the technique of 'pushing' the guitar strings with our fingers. This increases the tension on the string and causes the note we're playing to go up in pitch.

The two most common types of string bend are the tone or full step bend (bending the note up so that it sounds like the note 2 frets higher) and the semi-tone or half-step bend (bending the note to sound like the note 1 fret higher). Sometimes you'll see a 'tone and a half' bend (3 frets higher in pitch). The following example shows how you'll see these bends notated in guitar tab - always follow the notation accurately to get the bends sounding in tune!

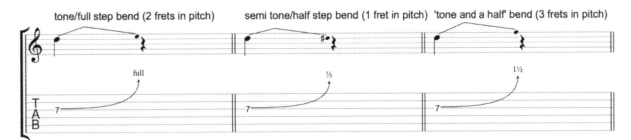

Bending Hand Position

Hand position is important when it comes to bending well. Let's look at some guidelines.

Thumb Over The Top

Controversial I know - but I believe you need your thumb solidly over the top of the neck when you bend. This gives you the grip, control and stability you need to master bending. If having your thumb over the neck feels awkward at first, don't cheat and let it slip behind - persevere until it feels natural. The chances are it will pay off big-time in the sound of your bends.

'Back Up' Bending Finger With Previous Fingers

When possible, use more than one finger to execute the bend. For example, when bending with your third finger, your first and second fingers should also be helping to push the string as demonstrated in **video 1.2**

There are certain situations when you may need to bend with one finger, but most of the time 'backing up' is the way to go. It not only gives you the pushing power you need to bend well, but also helps you keep your grip as you bend.

'Pin' the String As You Bend

It should feel like you are 'pinning' the string to the fretboard as you bend it. If you don't, you'll probably lose the note as you bend it. Again, watch **video 1.2** for a demonstration of this.

How To Bend

Once you've got the hand position you need, how do you actually execute the bend? This is the part that many people get wrong (including me when I started out) so let's make sure that you get off on the right track.

Rotate the Wrist

Many players try to bend by simply 'pushing the string up' with their fingers. You *can* move the string and get something resembling a bend this way, but it's definitely not the best method.

Instead, rotate the wrist to move the string. This gives you all the strength of your wrist and hand to move the string with, meaning better control and much better sounding bends.

Important: make sure to maintain the correct hand position *as you bend*. Some people *start* with their hand in the right place, but as soon as they start pushing the string to bend it their hand position collapses. Watch that this doesn't happen to you!

Push Up or Pull Down?

We can either push the string up (towards your head) or pull it down (towards your feet). Which should you use?

It depends, but as a general rule, bend the G, B and top E strings up towards your head. These are the most common strings to bend, so you'll be pushing the string up most of the time. You will see bends on the D, A and low E string as well, and with these it is best to bend them down towards your feet.

Sometimes you'll see someone deviate from these guidelines, but most of the time they work well. Remember that whether you're bending a string up or pulling it down the same technique guidelines apply.

That's Your Bending Crash Course...

Don't worry if this method of bending feels awkward to start with, it probably will take a while to feel natural. Keep checking you're not straying from the technique guidelines mentioned above as you work through this book, this will ensure that you develop a bending technique that does not let you down when you need it.

Final Thoughts on Technique

Hopefully these principles will help you fine-tune your basic playing technique and correct any bad habits you may have picked up. Throughout this book there are many more tips and lessons to help you expand your technical prowess on the guitar.

It's easy to become obsessed with guitar technique, but it's really just a tool for expressing your *musical ideas* effectively. Try to maintain this perspective, and don't make great playing technique become the *main* focus of your guitar playing. Some of the world's most popular guitar players don't have state-of-the-art playing technique, just enough to play music which connects with their audience. Ultimately it's the music you play that really matters, so try not to fall into the technique-trap that so many players (including myself) have fallen victim to at some time!

Quickfire Lesson: Your Soloing Vocabulary

Much of the focus in this book is on building a soloing vocabulary. We'll see all sorts of ways to do this, but first let's state what I mean by *soloing vocabulary*.

Your *soloing vocabulary* is the 'library' or 'toolkit' of musical ideas you use when you play guitar solos. The more you develop and learn to use your vocabulary, the more freedom you'll have to play the way you want to.

It's like learning to speak a language, Spanish for example. With a tiny vocabulary of Spanish words and phrases, you'll be very limited when having a conversation - you might *know* what you want to say, but you won't know *how* to say it. With a larger vocabulary you'll have more freedom to express opinions, respond to the other speaker, and communicate much more easily.

But it's not just the size of your vocabulary that matters. With just a moderate sized vocabulary plus an understanding of how to use it, you can speak to other people. On the other hand, knowing millions of Spanish words, but not knowing how and when to use them in conversation is useless.

So, we also need to learn what to do with our vocabulary, this largely comes from experimentation, practice and experience.

Some of the ways we build our soloing vocabulary are by:

- Learning the vocabulary of other players by copying their licks and solos
- Using the vocabulary of other players as a 'jumping off' point for our own ideas
- Transcribing (working out) other people's solos by ear
- Experimenting and 'messing about' to come up with licks and solos of our own
- Listening to music that inspires and ultimately may influence us
- Exploring and listening to our own musical imagination

I think that constantly developing our vocabulary should be one of our primary goals as guitar players, and this is precisely what this book will help you to do. By learning the licks, performing the practice tasks, and experimenting with the concepts you'll find in this book, your soloing vocabulary can't *help* but grow massively.

Just relax, do the work, and your vocabulary will take care of itself. This will in turn allow you to achieve greater freedom in your playing.

That's It For Now...

I think we're ready to begin. I'm really excited about what this book is going to help you to achieve, so grab your guitar and let's get started. Good luck, and see you in the next chapter!

Chapter 2:
Building Your Blues-Rock Lick Vocabulary

Early rock guitar was really the result of pioneers like Jimi Hendrix, Jimmy Page, Eric Clapton and Jeff Beck taking the licks and solos they heard on blues records and playing them with a new sound. The innovations of these and other players were mimicked and developed by successive generations of rock guitarists, and even today, a huge proportion of rock and metal guitar licks are simply blues licks played with the power, flair and energy integral to rock music.

Personally, I don't think you can sound authentic without a good range of blues based rock licks in your vocabulary, and this is exactly what this chapter is designed to give you.

We're also going to cover some powerful practice techniques as well as look at some more string bending tips. I think you'll be amazed at what you can do with the material presented in this chapter, so let's get started.

Working With 'Power Moves'

Learning licks by other players is one of the *best* things we can do to build a vocabulary and become an effective soloist. This process is how many, if not most, of the great rock players developed their way of playing.

But learning licks can be a trap and a time-suck. Many players tell me that no matter *how many* licks they learn, they feel like they can never remember or *use* them when they play a solo. It's no wonder that some people conclude that learning licks is a waste of time.

In my experience helping players who complain of this, the problem is normally that the licks they are learning are simply too *long*. I think that the best way to build vocabulary and fluency is by learning and experimenting with **very short** musical ideas. Short licks are:

- easy to learn
- easy to remember
- versatile and easy to work into your playing

I like to refer to short lick ideas as **power moves**. I call them this because they give musical tools like scales their 'musical power'. Power moves stop a scale from *sounding* like a scale - instead, they make it sound like music.

Power Moves

The English language might be based around the 26 letters in the alphabet - but we don't *consciously* use them when we have a conversation. We communicate our ideas using sentences and phrases built from **words**. Words are the 'building blocks' of language. We use words to express ourselves when we speak, we don't even think about the alphabet!

Think of power moves as **musical words**. Just as words are the building-blocks of sentences, power moves are like the building-blocks of licks and solos.

By experimenting with power moves you eventually go *beyond* thinking about tools like scale patterns when you play. Instead you'll base your ideas around the power moves contained *inside* the scale shape and all the possible things you can do with them. This can truly transform your playing.

The power moves approach is integral to this book - I'm going to show you how to use them to build a vocabulary, licks, and eventually your own guitar style.

Let's examine some power moves now, this will make this concept super clear.

For soloing in the key of C minor we'd likely use the C minor pentatonic scale. This is like our 'alphabet'.

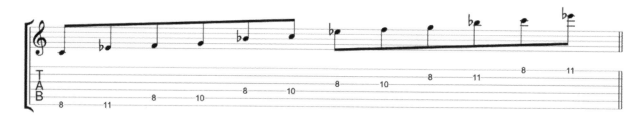

We can now hunt out power moves within the scale pattern, and use them to help us play things that make musical sense. Here are some possible power moves examples:

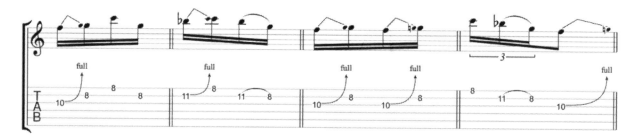

These power moves give you *ideas* or *clues* for *what* you might do when you use this scale to play a solo. Even better, power moves like these can be *combined* to come up with loads of different licks.

Eventually you'll find yourself doing this on-the-fly! You might find yourself playing a lick like the following - see how the power moves from a moment ago are in there?

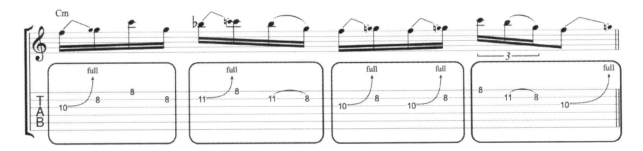

Important Point About Power Moves

It's **not** about learning hundreds of power moves which you then regurgitate in your solos.
Power moves *educate* you on *how* to use the scale musically. They show you things like which notes are good to bend and which note combinations can sound good together. Put another way, power moves help you discover the music which is hiding *inside* the scale. With time and deliberate practice, you'll **intuitively** make up your own musical ideas using what you learned *from* the power moves - what they taught you will become assimilated into your soloing vocabulary. This might not happen as fast as you'd like it to, but with the right kind of practice it will happen. So, what do I mean by the right kind of practice?

Practice Techniques for Faster Learning, Recall and Mastery

I suggest employing all of the following practice techniques as you work through this book - they *really* work. For demonstration purposes I'll apply these techniques to learning a simple power move, but you'll want to use these later to learn the longer lick and solo examples too.

Start by **memorising** the power move you want to work with. Don't hurry - take your time to get it in your memory and under your fingers. When you've done that use the following techniques to help you really nail it.

Embed

Study how the power move is **embedded** in the scale pattern. Don't see it as an isolated lick - see it as an idea within the *framework* of the scale pattern. Doing this means you'll be able to find and use it whenever you use the scale pattern, even when you move it into other keys.

Visualise

Look at your fretboard and **visualise** the power move. In other words, 'see' your fingers playing it without actually playing it. This is a *powerful* mental rehearsal technique, similar to methods used by many top performers and athletes.

Vocalise

Sing the power move along with your visualisation. This builds the connection between where it is on the fretboard and what it *sounds* like, drilling it deep into your memory, your musical 'ear', and your subconscious. How well you sing is *not* important, just get used to using your **voice** as the powerful but neglected practice tool that it is!

Play and Rest

When you're ready, play it along with some form of accompaniment like a backing track, a drum loop, or a metronome. Don't loop the power move continuously - use the **play and rest** approach: play it once, rest for one repetition, play it again, and repeat over and over.

The resting part is important, I find it stops me becoming fatigued and keeps me focused on the exercise instead of 'switching off', resulting in higher quality practice.

Make sure to employ all these techniques in your practice sessions. This multifaceted process might seem laborious, but will get you the results you want much sooner than a more haphazard approach. To see all these techniques quickly demonstrated see **Video 2.1 - Practice Techniques** (part of your free downloadable bonus content).

The 'Four Cs' of Practice

Sloppy practice will yield a sloppy result! Make sure to observe the 'Four Cs' of practice as you work through the power moves and other material in this book.

Control: play everything in a *controlled* way. This means the rhythm and timing is tight, bends, hammer-ons etc are played cleanly and accurately, and you're not rushing and making mistakes

Consistent: when playing a lick or exercise try to be consistent with things like fingering and picking. You'll get it together faster than if you use multiple variations which you then need to remember

Calm: it's easy to tighten up, hold your breath, or put your body into an awkward position when practicing new things. Tension is your enemy, so try to stay as calm, relaxed and as loose as possible

Commitment: even though you're only practicing, play everything with the commitment and energy you would if you were performing. This simple habit will have a big impact on the sound of your playing!

When you practice, check that you're following these guidelines - it will make your practice more productive, rewarding and fun. Ok, let's get into some power moves now...

Essential Blues-Rock 'Power Moves'

Time to learn some essential rock and metal power moves. You'll almost certainly hear these being used in the licks and solos of your favourite players. All these power moves are shown in the key of **D minor** and use the **shape 1, D minor pentatonic scale**. Suggested fingerings are given for each one, try them, they work well (more on fingering options soon).

If you're already using some of these power moves in your playing then great, you're on the way to building your vocabulary. This doesn't mean you should skip past this section though! There will almost certainly be ideas here which you *don't* already use - so work on these ones. Anyone can benefit from working with these power moves, so take as much as you can from these examples and find a way to use them to expand *your* vocabulary, whatever level it's at.

Note: all these power moves are demonstrated in **Video 2.2 - Essential Blues Rock Power Moves,** available in your free bonus download pack:

headstockbooks.com/rock

Common Bends

Let's start simple. These power moves show you the most common string bends. These might not look like much but you'll see them literally *everywhere* so make sure to nail them! Fingering is given but try a few other options as well to build your bending skills.

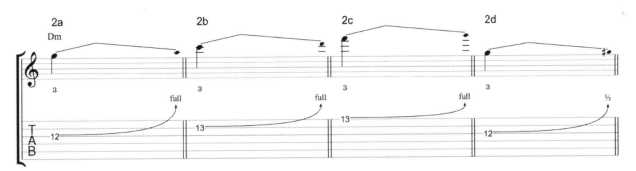

Bending Combinations

Let's combine these bends with other notes in the scale to get some useful ideas. Remember to check your bending technique using the guidelines from earlier as you work on all these examples (more on bending coming soon). Picking directions are shown - feel free to change these if you pick differently to me.

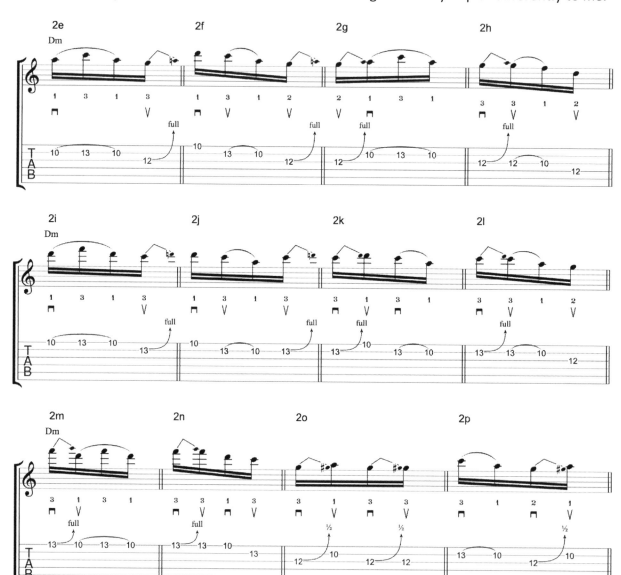

Multiple String Bends

This next set of power moves focuses more on bends. In some cases we're using several bends in the same power move.

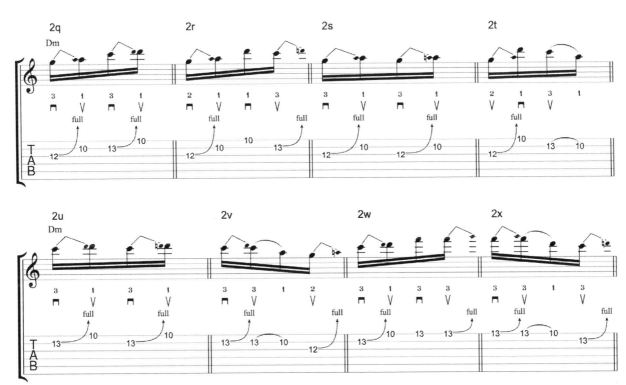

Examples **2s** and **2u** use **unison bends**. This is where the same pitch we bend the string to is also played on a neighbouring string. Even though the bent and unbent strings give you the same note - the sound of the string bend creates a cool effect. **Unison bends** are being used in many of the power moves we've seen so far - can you spot them?

Of course, there are *thousands* more power moves which are not covered here. I've focused on what I think are some of the most common and useful ideas, but feel free to create your own and add them in.

Power Moves Exercise

Try combining some of these power moves to get **5 licks** of your own (2-4 bars long each). Make sure to do this exercise, it will show you just how powerful these short ideas are for improving your soloing vocabulary. Try it and see for yourself, it wouldn't surprise me if you discover *dozens* of new ideas to use in your solos.

Don't overcomplicate your licks, simple but effective is the goal! Also, don't worry if some of the things you try don't work. Just keep going - the whole point is to experiment so that you *find out* what works and what doesn't.

One more thing: keep a written record of the best licks you discover. If you don't do this then there's a danger of forgetting them. If they're written out in tablature then it's easy to return and work them into your playing style - just like an artist uses a sketchpad to keep track of ideas they might develop later on. Use your **Blank Tab Practice Workbook** for this, it's part of your free download bonus content (see front of book for details).

That's it on power moves for now. In a moment I'll give you some longer licks which display elements found in these power moves - these will reinforce the logic of the approach we're taking here.

Quickfire Lesson: Is There a 'Best' Fingering for a Lick?

As you worked through the power moves you may have noticed I was sometimes using different fingers when playing the same idea. For example the G string bend played in power moves 2e and 2f. For 2e I'm using my 3rd finger, but for 2f I'm using my 2nd.

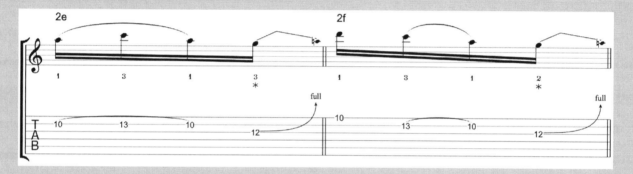

Learning to choose the best fingers to use for playing something is a very important skill to develop - but I don't think there is a 'best' way to finger a particular lick. The 'best' option depends on what you played before, what you're going to play next, where on the neck you're playing the lick and what your other fingers are doing. In my experience, being flexible with fingering is a good thing, so avoid dogmatically following 'rules' - they normally come with limitations. Of course, we should generally avoid any illogical, awkward, or inefficient fingerings!

For the examples in this book I'm showing fingerings which I find to work *most* of the time. I'm also slipping in some different fingerings at times **to help you become more flexible and versatile**. I believe that by following my suggestions your playing technique and fluency will improve.

In conclusion, follow and learn from my suggestions, but don't be afraid to change them to suit you - my way won't be the 'best' way to use in *every* situation.

10 Essential Blues-Rock Licks

The coming set of 10 licks demonstrate some ways to use ideas learned from the power moves to create some authentic rock and metal licks. You'll also see simple **scale fragments** being used.

Scale Fragments

A *scale fragment* is simply an ascending or descending chunk of a scale pattern. These can also be useful building-blocks to have in your vocabulary. The following examples are some simple minor pentatonic scale fragments shown in the key of D minor.

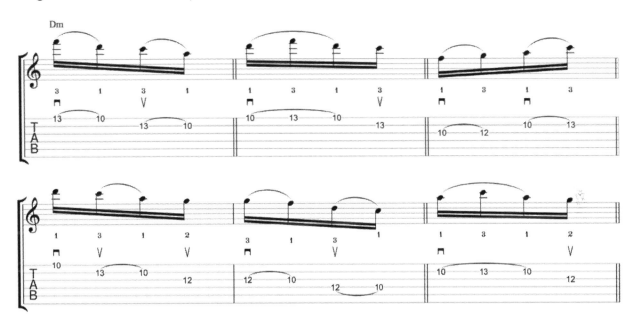

Here are some fragments using triplet rhythms. Remember to check out the **rhythm reading appendix** at the back of this book if you want to learn more about different rhythmic groupings.

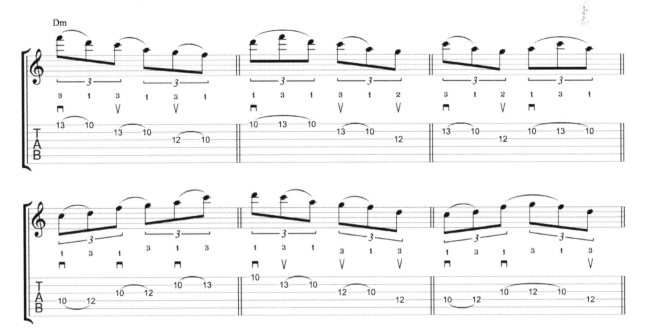

Look out for scale fragments like these as you work through the example licks coming up.

Ok, time for some licks. All these examples come from the shape 1 minor pentatonic scale, but look out for the *b*5th from the blues scale being added in places too. A variety of common rock keys are used to help you get used to playing in any key.

The licks have a 'star rating' of 1-4. This is designed to give you some idea of difficulty level. Licks with 1 star (*) are the easiest licks, those with 2, 3 or 4 stars are progressively more challenging. As you work through them, remember to follow and use the various practice tips and techniques from earlier - they'll make a big difference to the quality of your practice.

Picking and fingering directions are shown to indicate how I'd play these examples - hopefully these will help you to play them efficiently. Don't forget the **Lick Challenge** shown below each lick - doing these will help you get the most from learning these examples.

Also look out for some of the power moves from earlier in these licks and note how they're being used. Then, as soon as you're ready, try using these licks (or bits of them) in your own solos or improvisations. Enjoy!

(**Important**: See each of these licks demonstrated close up and at various speeds in **Video 2.3 Essential Blues Rock Licks**. This is part of your **free downloadable bonus pack** - see the front of this book to find out where to get it from!)

Lick 1 - I See DC *

This lick in the key of A minor uses a super-common G string bend plus a classic double-stop (2 notes played together). This kind of lick is typical of blues based rock players like Angus Young and shows the influence of early rock 'n' roll pioneers like Chuck Berry and Scotty Moore.

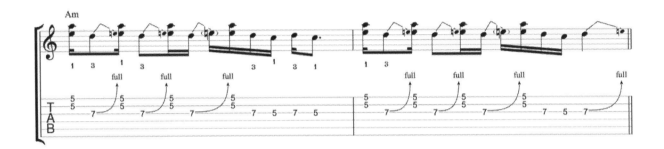

Here's your Lick Challenge

Can you create a new lick using the bend and double-stop manoeuvre which makes up most of this lick?

Write out any good ideas you discover so you don't forget them.

Lick 2 - Black Latin *

The following lick is based on the playing of Carlos Santana and is in the key of D minor. Carlos' fusion of blues, rock and Latin music has proved to be very popular, and many of his albums from the 1970's are still relevant today. Check out recordings like *Abraxus* and *Supernatural* to hear his tasty Latin-rock playing.

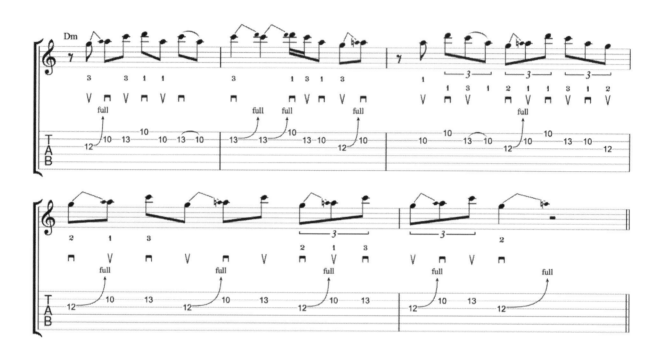

Here's your Lick Challenge

Once you know this lick, move it into the keys of E minor and C minor.

Lick 3 - Doubling Down *

This lick features standard pentatonic ideas which you'll hear most players use. Watch the timing of the bend and release move at the start of this lick and make sure to check the tuning of the half-step bend at the end of bar 2 (don't bend it too far up). Bars 3-4 introduce another double-stop idea for your soloing vocabulary. In bars 3-4 we're breaking with the alternate picking approach in order to play the double-stop with down picks - giving it more attack and power.

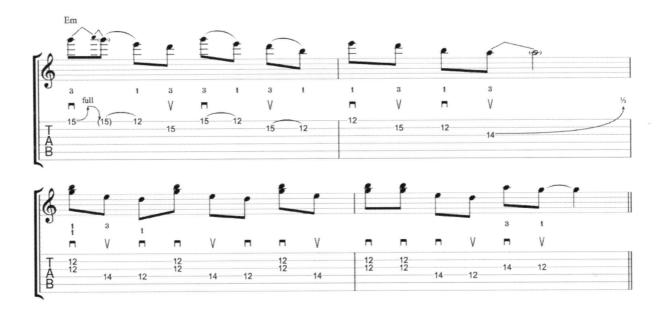

Here's your Lick Challenge

Take bar 1 of this lick. Can you create a few short licks of your own using the bend and pull-off moves it uses?

Lick 4 - Page Turner **

This lick in the key of A minor is the kind of thing Jimmy Page might play. It's a bit of a bend-fest! Aim to get the bend/release moves in bar 2 smooth, controlled, and in time - this will probably mean slowing it down so you can focus on what you're doing. Notice the use of unison bends in this lick too - a favourite device of blues influenced players like Jimmy (and virtually every rock player since).

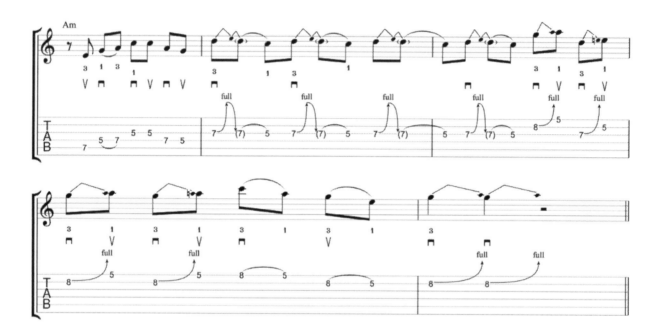

Here's your Lick Challenge

Move the A minor pentatonic scale pattern up 12 frets to the 17th fret. You can now play the scale and the lick an octave higher than shown in the example. The fingering should still work ok, although you might want to change it to allow for the spacing between the frets higher on the neck. Practice switching between the two octaves. Is this 'octave-switch' something you could use in your solos?

Lick 5 - Rock Stock **

Let's look at using triplets now. This lick in the key of C# minor employs many common rock triplet moves. I suggest following the fingering shown - it's probably the easiest way to play this example. Concentrate on getting the pull-off notes clean, articulate and in time - this will do wonders for your fretting hand technique.

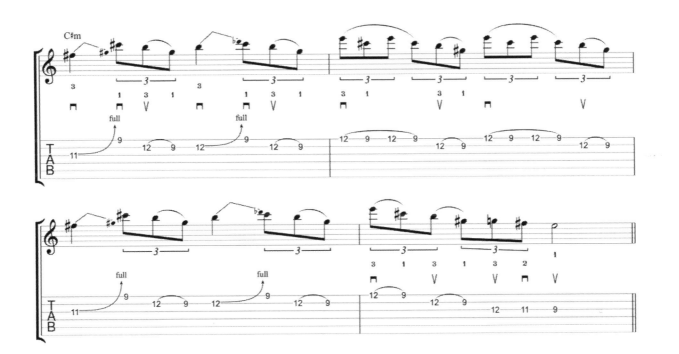

Here's your Lick Challenge

This lick can be broken up into 3 'chunks': bars 1&3, bar 2 and bar 4. Practice each chunk separately for a while to get it under your fingers. How could you combine them to get some new licks of your own? Find as many possibilities as you can and write down your favourites so that you don't forget them - they could be a cool addition to your soloing vocabulary.

Back for more licks in a moment - first, an important Quickfire Lesson!

Quickfire Lesson: Tidy Up Your Bends!

I want to quickly share some powerful tips to help you nail your string bending technique - it will have a big impact on how good you sound when you play. We'll be looking at bending again in chapter 3 - in the meantime, I hope these tips are helpful.

Tip 1 - 'Cut Off' Your Bends

Get used to silencing, or 'cutting off' your bends *before* you let them back down again. This stops you from hearing the string being released back to its original pitch. To do this, gently touch the string with your picking hand to mute it, then let the string down. You'll be amazed what a difference this simple tweak makes.

Sometimes we *want* to hear the string being let back down to its original pitch. In this case don't mute it - let the bent note continue to sound *as* you release it. The following lick illustrates these two concepts and the way they are written in the guitar tab.

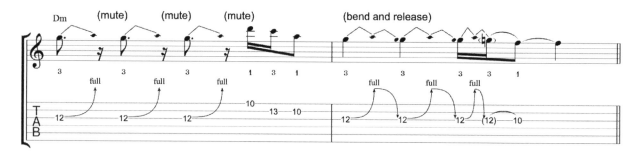

Tip 2 - Reach the Target Quickly

Try to get your bends up to pitch *quickly*. Many inexperienced players take too long to bend the string up, and you hear the incremental increases in pitch. Bending *straight up* to the target note (the note you're bending up to) sounds way slicker, so make sure to develop this skill.

Sometimes we *want* to hear the gradual increase in pitch as an effect, but the bottom line is this: make sure you are *in control* of how your bends sound, don't just leave it to chance.

Tip 3 - Mimic Other Players

Compare your bends to other players - how do they measure up? Are they tight, in time and controlled - or are they loose and noisy? Don't be *too hard* on yourself, bending takes time to master - but aim to get your bends sounding as good as the players you admire.

Lick 6 - Black Country**

Here's an E minor pentatonic lick based on the style of Black Sabbath guitarist Tony Iommi. The main challenge with this will probably be getting the bends controlled and nailing the rhythm at this speed. If you use the fingering shown then your 2nd finger needs to quickly hop from the D string to the G string towards the end of bar 2 (shown by * above picking indications).

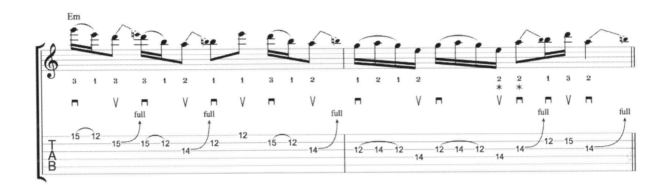

Here's your Lick Challenge

Move this lick into the key of D minor. Also work out how to play it in the keys of G minor and A minor above the 12th fret. The fingering shown should still work fine in these keys.

Lick 7 - Mike Strike **

This lick might remind you of German powerhouse Michael Schenker. As you study this example, notice how much repetition is used - the lick only uses a few ideas, they're just combined in a way that works. As always, focus on getting your bends accurate and the articulation of the notes clear - do this, and a lick like this can be a valuable soloing tool.

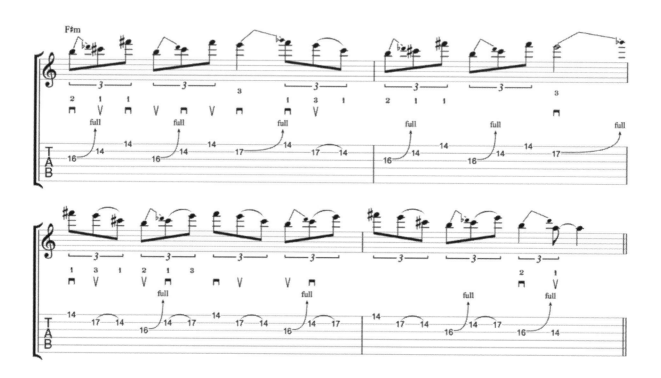

Here's your Lick Challenge

In bars 3-4, two simple triplet phrases are joined up to create a short but versatile lick. Isolate this part and practice looping it round and round. It's also a good idea to practice finding this idea in other keys.

Lick 8 - Unison Bender **

This lick focuses on playing unison bends over and over in quick succession. This will help you to refine your bending technique and build your stamina and strength. It also gives you some valuable soloing vocabulary, licks like this are an important part of the modern rock guitar style.

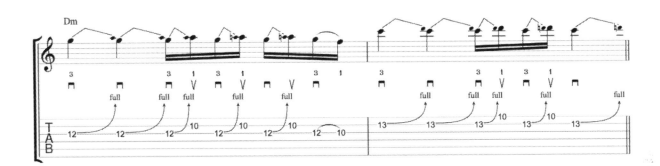

Here's your Lick Challenge

Can you take the simple bending ideas in this lick and use them to create some licks of your own? Experiment to see what you can come up with. Remember to practice *using* your new licks in a solo or over a jamtrack - this will really help you to make them part of your soloing vocabulary.

Lick 9 - Flat Fiver ***

Here we see the *b*5th interval from the blues scale being used to create a tasty soloing idea. Notice how we're using a 3rd finger slide to move between the 4th and the *b*5th intervals on the G string (at 12th and 13th frets respectively). This is a cool sounding move - steal it and use it in your solos! This lick is mostly built from 16th notes, be sure to get the timing crisp and clean.

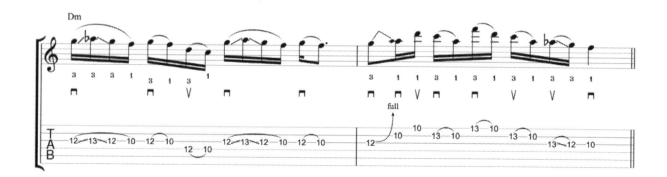

Here's your Lick Challenge

Isolate bar 1 of this lick and practice it round. Can you make up something of your own to play in bar 2? Create as many variations as you can - just experiment and use your imagination to see what you can discover!

Lick 10 - Wrapping Up ***

We'll end this chapter with a cool example in the key of E minor. By combining unison bends, scale fragments and blues scale ideas, we get a lick which is typical of players like Slash, Zakk Wylde, Randy Rhoads, Kirk Hammett and others. I find that the fingering and picking shown works great, but feel free to change it if you want.

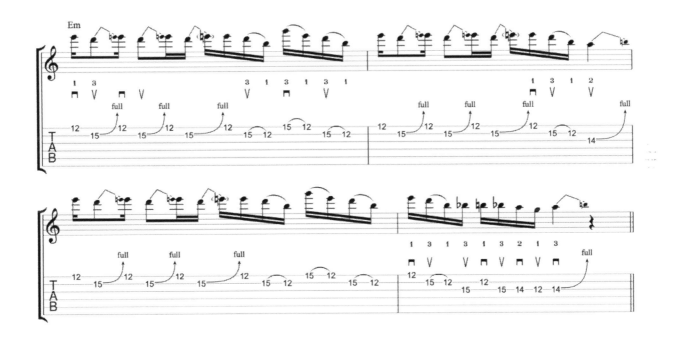

Here's your Lick Challenge

Move this lick into the keys of G minor, A minor, C# minor and D minor. Try it in G minor and A minor above the 12th fret as well.

Quickfire Lesson: Staccato and Legato

Two useful musical terms are **legato** and **staccato**.

Staccato describes a sound where each note has a clear 'attack'. *Legato* describes the sound of notes smoothly flowing together with less 'attack'.

On the guitar we can achieve a staccato feel by *picking* all or most of the notes in a lick, resulting in a more 'choppy' sound. If we use fretting hand techniques like hammer-ons, pull-offs and slides instead, we achieve a smoother, more legato sound.

Most of the examples in this book use some fretting hand techniques, giving them a more legato quality. I've done this because it is how *most* rock players tend to play licks like the ones I've given you. If you like a more staccato sound, then feel free to use *more* picked notes than I've shown in the examples - it's entirely up to you.

Most players use staccato *and* legato sounds, so experiment - with a little practice you'll find yourself going with whichever approach will work for the sound and mood you want to create.

That's All For This Chapter

I hope you've enjoyed working through this chapter and that the method and ideas I've shown you have yielded some good results.

I suggest working on the material in this chapter for a while longer - you can do a huge amount with it, and extra study time will pay off in a whole host of ways. Don't just play the power moves and licks I've shown you in a superficial way - explore them, get them under your skin, and make them a part of **your** playing!

Above all, be patient, and concentrate on mastering the essentials as you work on this material. Things like rhythm, timing, and the tuning of your bends can really make or break your playing - yet many players neglect them in favour of 'sexier' topics. Nobody becomes a great rock soloist overnight, just try to practice consistently, adding new ideas to your playing bit by bit - and you'll see a big shift over time.

Good luck, and when you do feel ready for more I'll see you in the next chapter.

Ready To Move On?

- Do you understand the idea of power-moves and how we can use them to build a soloing vocabulary?

- Have you learned some power moves and practiced using them?

- Are you following all the practice guidelines and using some of the methods described? Are they working for you?

- Have you learned from studying the sample licks? Have they given you new soloing ideas you can use?

If the answer to these questions is yes, and you honestly feel like you're ready to move on - great work! Head to Chapter 3.

Chapter 3:
More Essential Blues–Rock Licks

In the previous chapter you started building a core vocabulary of blues based rock style licks. To do this you worked with short musical phrases we called **power moves**. You also learned some blues-rock licks similar to ideas heard in the solos of many rock guitar greats. If you did the tasks I set for you (and I hope you did!) then you will have seen how everything studied can be used to create authentic rock licks of your own.

In this chapter we're going to build on everything you learned in those lessons. We'll see more advanced power moves, how to use them to create licks, as well as study some crucial vibrato and string bending techniques. When you add everything from the previous chapter to what you'll learn in this one, you can create some pretty awesome rock and metal guitar licks and solos!

Ok, let's get started by looking at a crucial technique you need in your armoury if you want to play solos which really make an impact: **vibrato**.

Vibrato Technique

Note: Watch **Video 3.1 - Vibrato Technique** to see these techniques, principles and exercises demonstrated up close. This video is part of your free bonus download pack (details in front of book).

Vibrato is the technique of making a note 'shake' or 'wobble' in pitch to give it more expression, and it's one of the most powerful tools in the rock player's toolkit. Vibrato is shown in music notation and guitar-tab by a wiggly-line written above the note in question. You can see this in two places in the following lick:

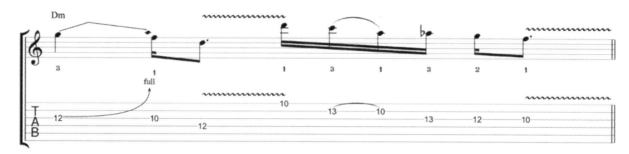

Just like with bending, *how* we execute vibrato has a big impact on the resulting sound, so let's look at some important vibrato guidelines. Even if you're familiar with using vibrato, check your technique alongside these guidelines - you may be able to improve the sound of it dramatically.

How To Get Vibrato On Guitar

By bending a string and letting it back down several times in quick succession a vibrato effect is created. For this reason vibrato technique is similar to bending technique.

In general, most rock players use a 'wide' vibrato style, where the note changes noticeably in pitch. This gives a more aggressive, energetic sound compared to a narrow, shallow vibrato. Listen to a player like Zakk Wylde to hear an awesome rock guitar vibrato. With good vibrato technique, patience and practice, you'll be able to achieve a similar sound in your playing.

Hand Position For Vibrato

The bending hand position we looked at earlier gives the strength and control needed for a good vibrato. A brief reminder of the key points:

- Keep your **thumb solidly over the top of the neck**. This provides the grip, control and stability you need to add vibrato to a note
- **'Back up'** the finger performing vibrato. An exception to this is when we vibrato with our first finger - in this case there are no previous fingers to back up with!
- **'Pin' the string.** Keep pressing the string *into* the fretboard to keep the note sustaining as you add vibrato to it

How To Vibrato

Just like with bending, pin the string firmly with your finger and **rotate your wrist** to move it. Then move your wrist back again to where it started, causing the note to return back to its starting position. Doing this several times without stopping causes the note to keep rising and falling in pitch, creating the vibrato effect.

Grab any note on the guitar and vibrato it, persevering until you hear a noticeable change in pitch. Don't worry if the change in pitch is only small, just make sure you're using the technique described here.

(**Reminder:** Make sure to watch **Video 3.1** to help all this vibrato stuff make sense!)

'Push' and 'Pull' Vibrato

Strings can be moved in an upward or downward motion to get vibrato. *Push vibrato* is where we push the string upwards towards our head and *pull vibrato* is when we pull the string downwards towards our feet. Which is used depends on which string you are playing. As a *general* rule:

- Use **push vibrato** on the **top E and B strings**
- Use **pull vibrato** on the **D, A and low E strings**

- On the **G string**, either can work so experiment. Personally, I tend to use pull most of the time - but it depends on the situation and which finger I'm using

Try these short licks to practice your vibrato. Follow the fingering and instructions shown for this. These licks are all in the key of D minor but make sure to move them to other keys as well.

Exercises 1-4 focus on your 1st and 3rd finger vibrato technique.

Vibrato Exercise 1

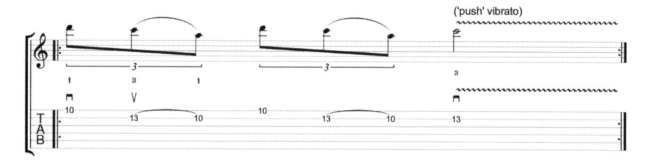

Vibrato Exercise 2

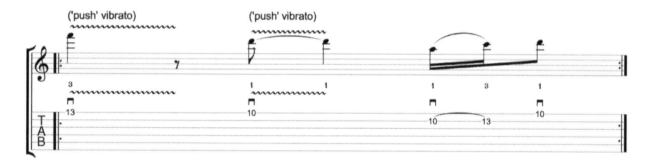

Vibrato Exercise 3

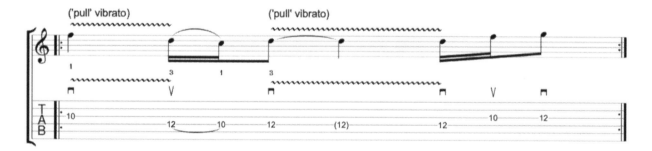

Vibrato Exercise 4

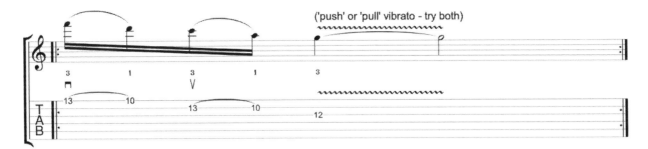

Exercise 5 will develop your 2nd finger vibrato chops.

Vibrato Exercise 5

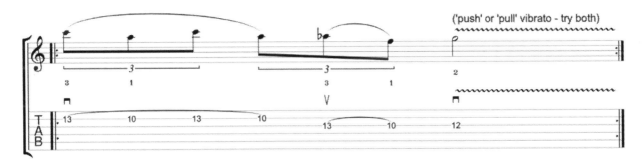

Personally I hardly ever vibrato with my 4th finger, but I can do it when I need to. Exercise 6 is a good exercise for building this skill.

Vibrato Exercise 6

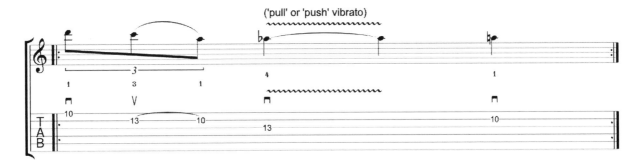

3 Vibrato Mistakes To Avoid!

Mistake 1: No Rhythmic 'Pulse'

Aim to make your vibrato *rhythmic*. You don't want to hear an out of control 'wobble', a good vibrato sounds more like a rhythmic pulsing. Slow your vibrato down and get the rhythm under control.

Mistake 2: Random Pitch Changes

With each cycle of vibrato (bend and release movement) aim for a similar fluctuation in pitch. If it's inconsistent and erratic, then you're not developing the control you need.

Mistake 3: Vibrato Sounds Out of Tune

The note you're adding vibrato to needs to go all the way *back to its original pitch* at the end of each vibrato cycle. Sometimes people hold it 'in between' the bend and the release because it feels easier. This makes their vibrato sound like an out of tune bend. Let the string all the way back to its *starting point* when you release it.

Nobody gets great vibrato technique overnight, it takes time to develop and feel natural - but it's important to listen to and critique your vibrato so that it starts to sound the way you want it to. Make sure to do this as you use vibrato in the examples in this book.

More Power Moves

In the previous chapter we looked at the concept of **power moves** and how we can use them to build our soloing vocabulary. In this lesson I'll show you some more advanced ideas, then later in this chapter we'll look at some licks which combine some of these.

All these power moves are using the D minor pentatonic and D blues scales, but remember, it's super-important to become fluent at playing them in other keys as well - don't neglect this vital skill. Also don't forget to use the practice methods and tips we covered in chapter 2, they'll help you get these ideas into your vocabulary.

Ok, grab your guitar and let's get started.

Note: all these power moves are demonstrated in **Video 3.2 - More Power Moves,** available in your free bonus download pack

Double Stop Bends

The following power moves demonstrate some useful double-stop bends. This is when we play 2 notes and bend one or both of them. These can create some powerful sounding rock licks.

When playing these, check you are only bending the required string - it's easy to accidentally bend both strings! It will take some practice to build up the required strength to do this but persevere. Following the fingerings shown will help.

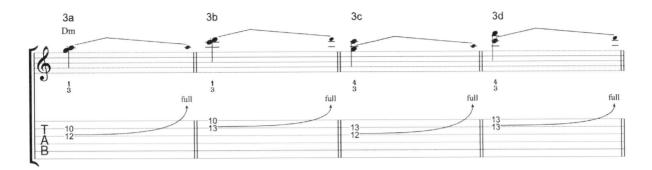

Sextuplet Power Moves

A *sextuplet* is like two 8th note triplets condensed into a *single beat*. For example, imagine we had the following idea:

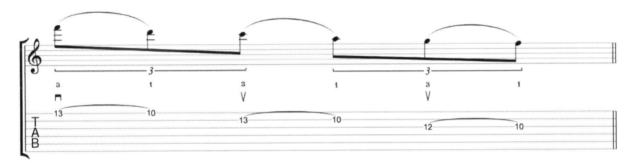

Played in this way, this phrase is 2 beats long. By playing it twice as fast we can 'squash' it into 1 beat instead. When we do this, it no longer uses 8th note triplets - it is built from 16th note triplets or sextuplets. Virtually all the triplet power moves from chapter 2 can be changed in this way.

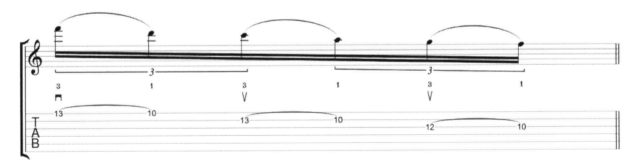

Working through the following power moves will help you become used to hearing and using sextuplets - notice how some of them are simply 'squashed' versions of triplet power moves from earlier. All are shown in the key of D minor.

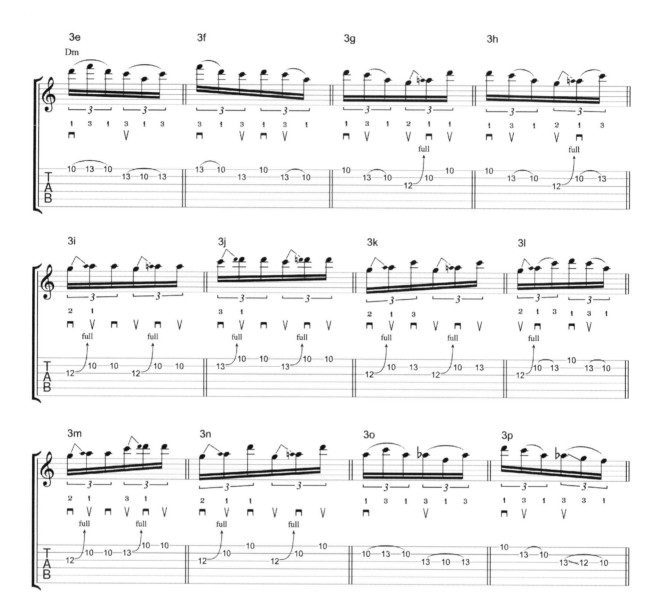

Here are some useful phrases which combine 8th notes and sextuplets. Remember, if any of these rhythmic concepts are confusing then see **Appendix 2: Rhythm Reading Basics** for help.

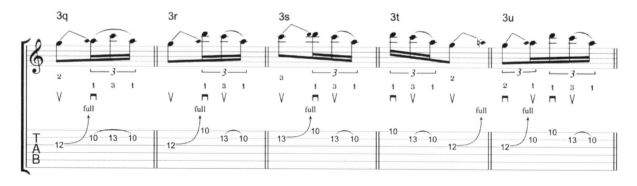

Power Moves Exercise

Time to have fun with some of these new power moves. Try combining some of them to get **5 licks** (each 2-4 bars long). Mix in some of the power moves from chapter 2 if you want - just try and come up with some ideas you can use.

As before, don't over complicate your licks, and remember to keep a written record of the best ones you discover. Of course, there are many other power moves which are not shown here - perhaps you can find some of your own and add them in? Have fun!

Quickfire Lesson: Bending Variations

In this short lesson we're going to look at a couple of common types of string bends - some of which you'll be seeing in the licks we're going to study shortly. I've deliberately avoided these bends so far in this book to give you a chance to get to grips with the basic bending technique - but now that you're familiar with that, let's dive into them.

Note: The examples in this lesson are demonstrated in **Video 3.3 - Bending Variations,** available in your free bonus download pack.

The Pre-Bend

With a pre-bend we don't hear the sound of the string being bent up - it's bent silently up to the target pitch, and only *then* is it picked. In most cases the bend is then released, giving the sound of the note returning to its original, un-bent pitch. Try the following exercise. Remember, bend the string silently, *then* pick it, then let it back down.

Example 1

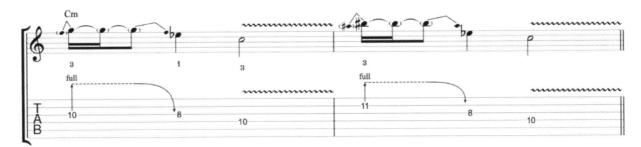

The next example shows some pre-bends being used in the context of a longer lick. See the Technique Tips that follow the example to help you execute it well.

Example 2

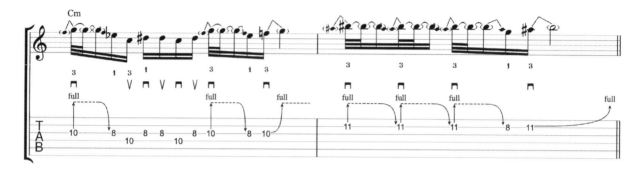

Technique Tips

1. Slow this example down as much as you need to in order to get it accurate and controlled. Rushing will result in haphazard pre-bending technique
2. As you release the bend, pin the string firmly against the fretboard to prevent the note fading out
3. Follow the picking directions. This will make sure the picking hand is not compensating for any weak pre-bends - your fretting hand wants to be doing most of the work here!

Quick Exercise: Put on a backing track of your choice and spend **5 minutes** experimenting with how you can use pre-bends in your solos. Try out all sorts of different ideas with the technique.

Repeated Bend and Release

This can be a really expressive technique to use in your solos. The basic idea is to play a series of bend and release movements, manipulating the pitch of the string as you do so.

Study the following example. In the 1st bar we're playing a simple picked melody from the C minor pentatonic scale. In the 2nd bar we're playing the same melody but the notes are created using string bending.

Example 3

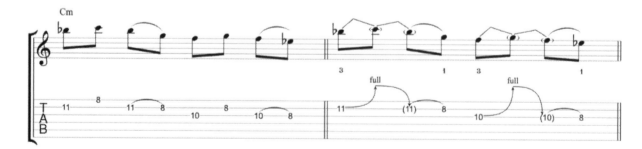

You can hear how the string bending version creates a smoother, more vocal sound - something we can use to great effect in our solos.

Here this idea is incorporated into a longer lick in the key of C minor. Notice how few pick strokes are used in the 2nd bar - most of the work is done by the fretting hand. After you've checked out the lick, experiment with how you can use this bending technique in your playing. See the technique tips that follow the example to get it sounding smooth.

Example 4

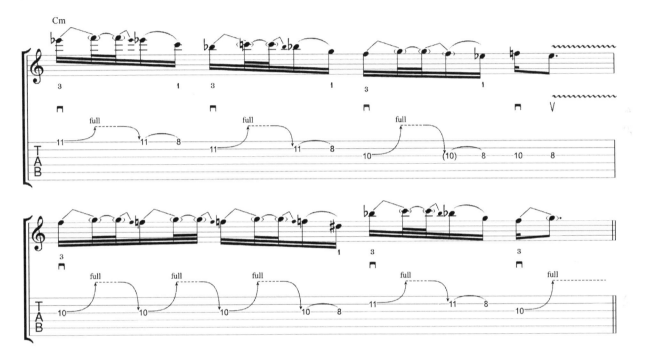

Technique Tips

1. Pin the string tightly against the fretboard during the bend **and** the release. If you don't then you'll lose the note

2. This lick takes a good degree of bending strength and control. Be patient and work on small sections at a time if you find the example difficult at first

3. Follow the picking indications shown here. This will force you to use your fretting hand to play the lick- resulting in you learning this powerful bending skill

Quick Exercise: Put on a backing track of your choice and spend **5 minutes** experimenting with how you can use this string bending approach in your playing. This will help to make it a part of your increasingly varied playing vocabulary.

Re-Picked Bends

Another common technique to try out is re-picking a bend. Try it now: simply bend any string, hold the bend up, and pick it repeatedly. You'll probably recognise the sound of this popular bending technique. The following example in C minor demonstrates this approach. Follow the picking indications as you hold the bend. Remember to check out **Video 3.3 - Bending Variations** to see this lick demonstrated up close.

Example 5

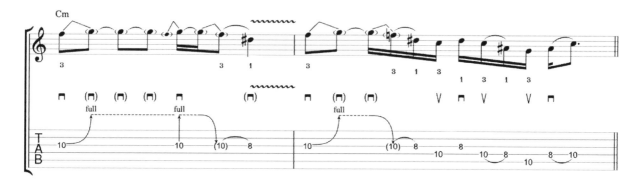

Another common approach is to pick the string repeatedly *as you bend it up*. This gives you the sound of the note gradually increasing in pitch and can be very effective. The following example begins with this idea. It's hard to appreciate the sound of this just from reading the tab, so make sure to check out **Video 3.3 - Bending Variations** to hear this example. Also notice the pre-bend midway through bar 1.

Example 6

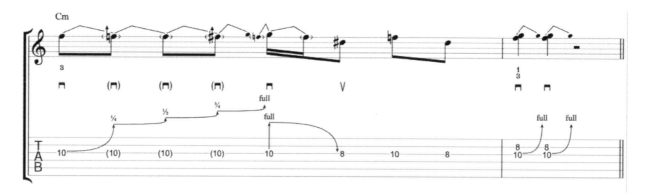

It can also sound great when we do the opposite: pick a bend as we slowly *release* it. Experiment with this idea on your own!

Technique Tips

1. Remember to 'pin' the bend firmly so that you don't lose the note (otherwise you'll be re-picking nothing)
2. Re-picked bends tend to sound best when you attack the string quite hard - don't be afraid to dig in!
3. When re-picking a string as you bend it up or release it, the change in pitch should be controlled and even throughout. Watch me demo the previous example to hear this - then practice getting it sounding the same way. This is great for developing your bending control

Quick Exercise: Put on a backing track of your choice and spend **5 minutes** experimenting with re-picking a bend as you hold it. Also try picking the string as you bend it up or release it.

10 More Essential Blues-Rock Licks

Let's look at working the techniques and power moves from this chapter into some authentic licks now. Just like the licks in chapter 2, these licks come from the shape 1 minor pentatonic scale, (sometimes with the b5th added) and use various common rock keys.

These licks are more challenging than the licks in chapter 2 - so be patient as you work on them. Remember to focus on the essentials: things like timing and rhythm, accuracy of bends, clarity of the notes etc - without these in place, you're not going to get these licks sounding as good as you want them to sound. As before, use the **star rating** as a guide to the difficulty of these examples.

Picking and fingering directions are shown, and remember to do the **lick challenges** given below each example. Also make sure that you are applying the practice methods and techniques we examined in chapter 2, they really work and I suggest making it a habit to use them.

As usual, try using bits of these licks in your guitar solos and improvisations when you feel ready. Ok, let's get into the examples.

(**Important**: You can see each lick demonstrated at various speeds in **Video 3.4 More Essential Blues Rock Licks**. This is part of your **free downloadable bonus pack** - see the front of this book for details)

Lick 1 - Jimi, Jimi ***

This lick in C# minor is inspired by Jimi Hendrix and uses some of his trademark double-stop bends. Can you spot some of our power moves in this lick?

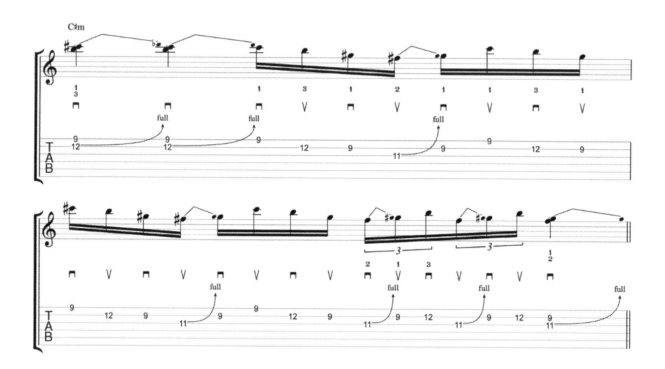

Here's your Lick Challenge

Use the ideas presented in bar 1 of this lick to make up 1-3 licks of your own. Doing this will help you get comfortable with using these ideas in your playing. Remember to write out any good licks you discover.

Lick 2 - Black 'n' Blue ***

This example is inspired by the playing of Angus Young. There's a lot going on here, so patiently work through it in small chunks before attempting to join it all together. Also pay attention to the suggested fingerings, especially the 3rd/4th finger manoeuvre halfway through bar 1.

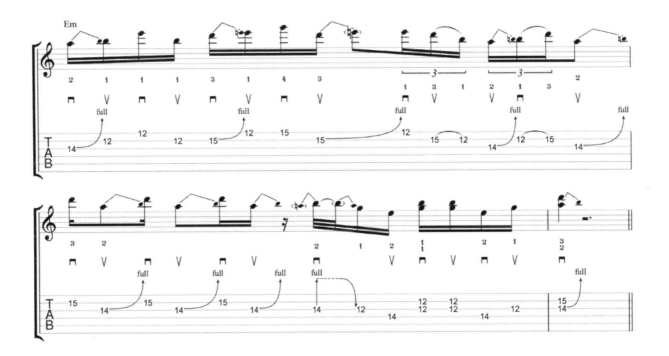

Here's your Lick Challenge

This lick is *rammed* full of essential rock soloing ingredients and is well worth some in-depth study. Highlight some of the bits you like most in this lick, then use them as ideas for creating some licks of your own. If you want to be really thorough, transpose your new licks into some other common rock keys like A minor, D minor, G minor etc.

Lick 3 - Appetite ***

You may have heard players like Slash play licks like this one. The example is in the key of E minor and uses a couple of the bending power moves from earlier in this chapter. It's quite simple and repetitive but will still take a fair amount of strength and stamina to get up to speed.

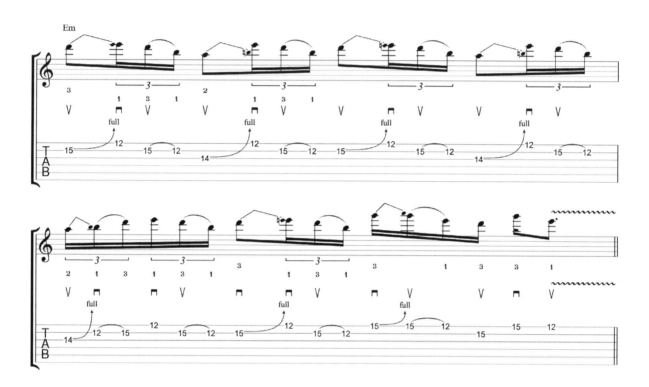

Here's your Lick Challenge

Can you find the key components making up this lick? (Hint: most of them are in bar 1). How could you recycle them to get a new lick? Perhaps you could change the order that they're played in? Experiment with these and other concepts to create some similar licks of your own. Don't be tempted to over complicate this process - I've found that keeping my ideas simple and stripped-down normally yields better results!

Quickfire Lesson: Adding Vibrato To String Bends

One way to make your bends really sing (or scream!) is to add vibrato to them. This is something you hear great rock guitarists do all the time, but many players struggle with this technique. Let's look at how it's done.

Don't think about holding the bend and adding vibrato to it. Instead, think about *letting the bend down very slightly, then bending it back up again*. Try this now on a couple of familiar string bends, persevering if it feels awkward at first - you'll get it with slow, controlled practice.

All the vibrato guidelines from earlier in this chapter apply when vibratoing a bend, so check your timing, tuning etc. Remember, we only want to let the bend down a *tiny* bit before pushing it back to the pitch of the bend.

Practice using this technique where indicated in the next batch of licks coming up now. Also check out the close up shots of me performing this technique in demonstration **Video 3.4 More Essential Blues Rock Licks**.

Lick 4 - Magic Man ***

Here's a great example of how to combine some blues scale ideas for a high-impact lick. Notice how the use of repetition gives the lick a sense of structure - something you could experiment with in your own licks perhaps? The final bar uses a double-stop bend we haven't seen yet - add it to your repertoire of double-stop power moves. By the way, this lick is based on the style of the great Zakk Wylde - enjoy!

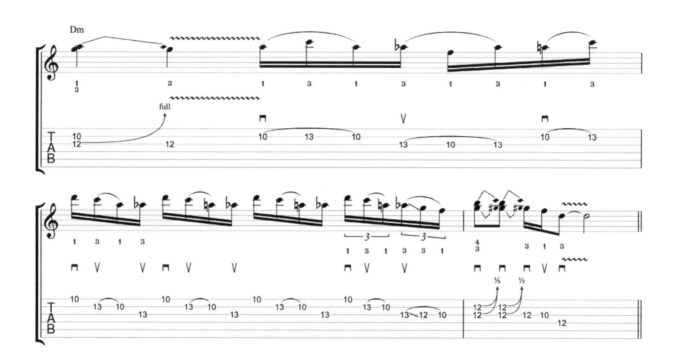

Here's your Lick Challenge

Move this lick into the key of G minor down at the 3rd fret. It may seem difficult, but try to maintain the fingering shown- the stretching practice will be great for expanding your fretting hand reach. Also practice playing the lick an octave higher.

Lick 5 - Dr Rock ***

This example in the key of C minor uses a familiar rock'n'roll idea in bar 1. Notice how this idea starts at different places each time it is played - it isn't always beginning on the beat. This creates a rhythmic 'overlapping' effect which probably sounds familiar. In bar 2 a descending 3-note-pattern works its way down the C minor pentatonic scale shape. Playing a repeating pattern (often called a **scale sequence**) through a scale shape in this way is a very common trick.

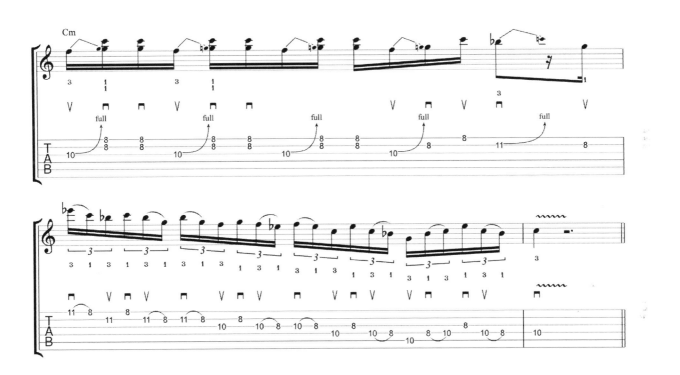

Here's your Lick Challenge

Change the double-stop phrase in bar 1 to generate some new licks. You could try playing more/less repetitions on the double-stop, change the rhythm, play the bend more times - there are loads of possibilities. Also look at bar 2. Can you see the sequence and how it is being used here?

Lick 6 - Diggin' Billy ***

This lick is inspired by Billy Gibbons and will give your bending technique a good workout. In bar 1 we've got a held and re-picked bend played in quarter note triplet rhythm. Notice how the bend is gradually let down towards the end of the bar. The pre-bend that starts the 2nd bar is followed by some common blues ideas - try to include the vibrato on the short bend at the end of bar 2. Finally, the lick finishes on a cool double stop bending move. This lick is slower than some previous examples - the challenge here is nailing those bends. Good luck!

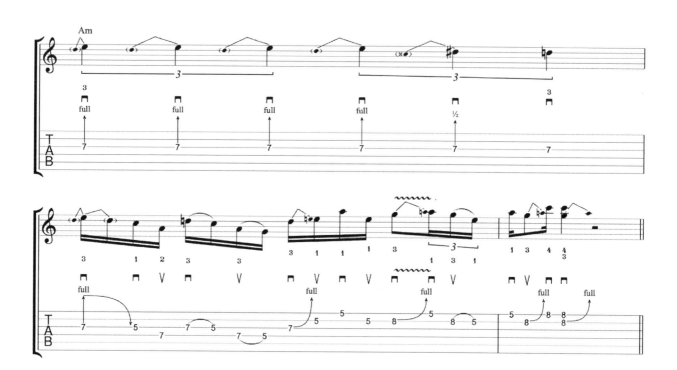

Here's your Lick Challenge

Extract the re-picked bend in bar 1, the pre-bend in bar 2, and the double-stop bend which closes the lick. These are 3 powerful bends to have in your soloing arsenal! Create some of your own licks using some or all of these bending ideas. Of course, you can add in other notes from the scale too.

Lick 7 - Sharp Shooter ****

This speedy lick is typical of 80's rock guitarists like Randy Rhoads and Michael Schenker. There are a few things to test you here, so work on the lick slowly, giving yourself the chance to build the required skills and speed to execute it well. I recommend using the fingerings given - I think they represent how most rock players would approach a lick like this. This example also affords you some great opportunities to practice applying vibrato to your string bends. Enjoy…

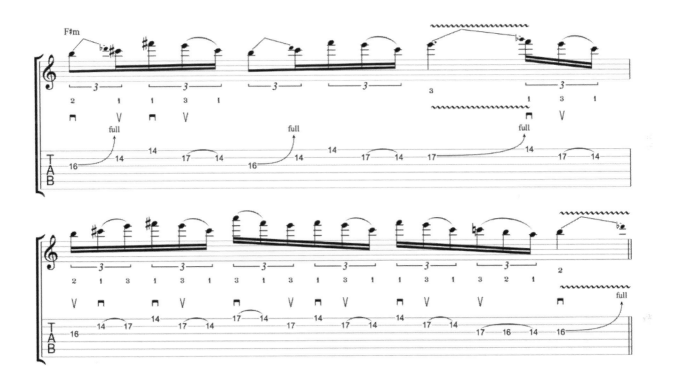

Here's your Lick Challenge

Keep the 1st bar of this lick the same, but create some alternative things you could play in the 2nd bar. Using a lick as a jumping-off point in this way is a great exercise for kickstarting your creativity! You could also reverse the exercise - keeping bar 2 and writing a new 1st bar. Move the exercise around some other keys as well to build flexibility using these ideas.

Lick 8 - Kinda' Country ****

This versatile example would sound right-at-home in a country rock song. There's nothing really new here, but executing this lick accurately might test you. As usual, slow everything down and gradually work on developing the necessary control and strength. I recommend using the fingering given for this example - it'll help you to build your bending chops.

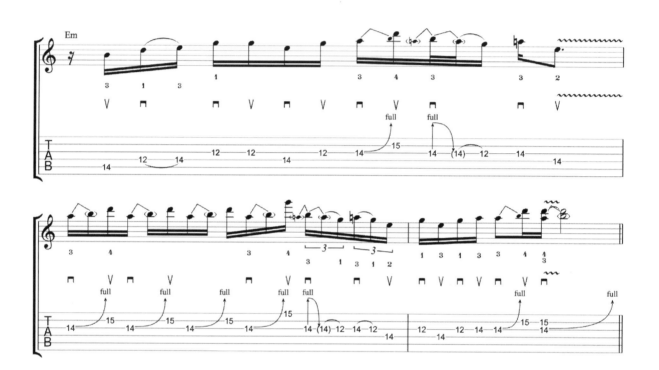

Here's your Lick Challenge

Transpose this lick into the keys of D minor, C# minor and C minor. Then play it in the key of A minor in both available octaves. The fingering should work fine in these keys too, but feel free to change things if necessary.

Lick 9 - Rat-Run ****

This lick begins with some wide bending vibrato, reminiscent of 80's players like Warren DeMartini and George Lynch. In bar 2 we've got a fast blues scale phrase. The 3rd finger needs to 'roll' between the G and B strings towards the end of bar 2 - also watch the picking here, the string-crossing can be a challenge. I think the fingering works great, but as always, modify it if you wish.

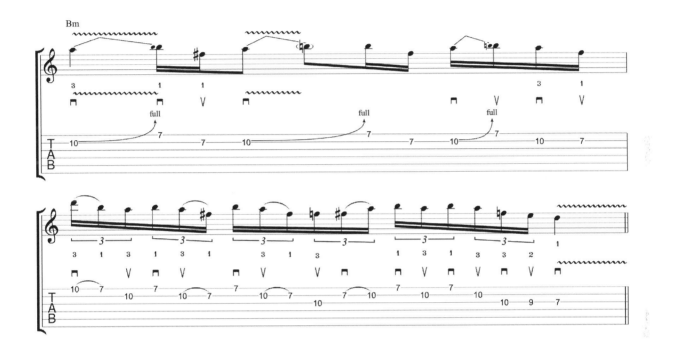

Here's your Lick Challenge

Experiment with the vibrato bend move in bar 1, using it as the central idea for some new licks. As before, don't over complicate things - just add a few notes to the bend to create some licks which sound good to you. You can also experiment with applying some different rhythmic ideas to the bend - just follow your creativity and go with what sounds good to you.

Lick 10 - Shift It ****

This lick begins with a simple pentatonic pull-off move. This is followed by a repeated bend/release move which will test your bending strength and control, especially this low down on the fretboard! Notice how the bend is only picked once, the rest of the work is done by the fretting hand.

In bar 2 we rapidly shift up an octave to end with an edgy little blues scale phrase. The sudden position shift halfway through this example could easily catch you out - follow the fingering shown, it makes it much easier. I also find that looking where I want to move to shortly *before* the position shift helps me end up in the right place - try this for yourself.

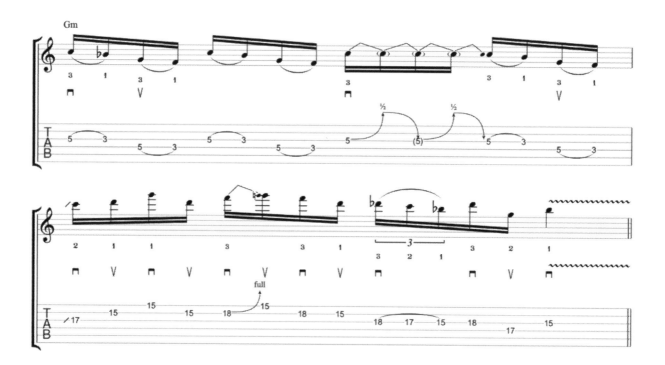

Here's your Lick Challenge

Practice working some 'octave shifts' into some licks of your own - it can be a simple but powerful trick, creating an element of surprise for the listener. This will work best in keys like G minor, A minor or F# minor - in some other keys you may run out of frets. Experiment with using this rapid octave-shift technique in your soloing over a backing track too.

That's All For This Chapter

Congratulations on reaching the end of this chapter - hopefully you're really beginning to see a transformation in your playing skills and your ability to play authentic rock ideas on the guitar.

It's probably a good idea to further study the material in this chapter before moving on. This will help you to really soak it up into your playing. I truly believe that if you can effectively use what we've covered so far in this book, you can sound like a fantastic guitarist. Don't be in a hurry, investing extra time will pay off.

So dig into it, and when you're ready I'll see you in the next chapter. Good luck!

Ready To Move On?

- Are you on the way to developing a good vibrato technique?

- Have you explored the bending techniques we've examined (pre-bends, re-picked bends etc)?

- Have you learned and practiced using the power moves in this chapter?

- Are you getting comfortable with adding vibrato to string bends?

- Have you learned from studying the sample licks and developed new soloing ideas from them?

If the answer to these questions is yes, and you're genuinely ready to move on - great work! Continue to the next chapter!

Chapter 4:
'Deep Trouble' Solo Study, Pinch Harmonics and More!

In this chapter we're going to look at the *Deep Trouble* solo study. This will give you an idea of how to put some of the ideas covered so far together into a complete solo. This chapter is also designed to break up the intensity of this book, and just give you something fun to play around with! I'll take you step-by-step through the solo and give you all sorts of useful performance tips to make sure that studying it is a beneficial and useful exercise.

We're also going to look at how to increase your fluency and playing speed, plus study another essential rock technique: **pinch harmonics**. So, let's get started.

Pinch Harmonics and How To Do Them

Rock players use **pinch harmonics** to produce a 'squealing' sound on their guitar. This might sound like a weird thing to want to do, but it's become a staple of the rock guitar sound. It's also a topic people ask about a lot, so in this lesson I'll give you the essentials you need to make your guitar 'squeal' at will!

Note: Watch **Video 4.1 - Pinch Harmonics** to see the technique demonstrated up close. This video is part of your free bonus download pack (details in front of book).

Pinch Harmonic Technique

The **pinch harmonic** technique is not the *only* method for generating the sound of harmonics on the guitar, but it's the one rock players seem to use the most.

To get a pinch harmonic, catch the string with the side of your thumb *immediately* after picking it. This should feel like a *single* movement - almost like you're picking the string with the pick *and* the side of your thumb at the same time. It's challenging to explain the pinch harmonic technique in a book, so make sure to watch the accompanying video demonstration to see it up close.

The following exercise will help you learn to execute this technique. I suggest using a bit of distortion for this - it makes it easier to bring the harmonics out.

1. Play the G string at the 5th fret
2. Using small down picks, pick slowly along the length of the string between the end of the fretboard and the bridge of your guitar, working your way along the string. Remember, catch the string with the side of your thumb as you pick it!
3. Hopefully you'll hear the sound of the string plus a higher note too - this is the harmonic
4. Don't worry if you don't get it at first, keep going, adjusting the technique to get results

With a bit of trial and error you should start to get the pinch harmonic coming out clearly. A few things to help:

1. The harmonic is easier to get when picking at some points on the string than others. Picking at different places along the string helps us get a feel for the harmonic 'sweet spots'
2. With practice, you'll instinctively get a feel for where to pick the string in order to get a harmonic. Don't over analyse this process, just experiment, trusting that the technique will come with practice
3. You need the side of your thumb to be close to the edge of the pick. If it's not then it's harder to 'nick' the string with your thumb as you pick. You may find that you need to slightly modify how you grip the pick

Vibrato, Bending and Harmonics

Pinch harmonics really start to come alive when we add vibrato and bends to them. Here's a short lick in the key of A minor to get you started with adding vibrato to a pinch harmonic. Notice how 'PH' (for pinch harmonic) is written above the note in the tab. There are other ways of notating pinch harmonics, but we'll be using this method. All the vibrato guidelines from earlier still apply when adding vibrato to a pinch harmonic.

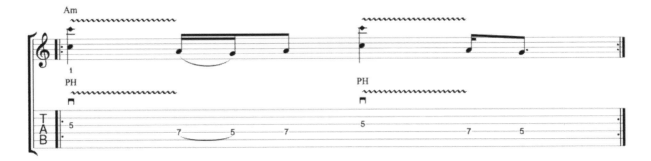

In the next example we're adding a pinch harmonic to a bend. Don't overthink this: simply pick the string to get a harmonic, then bend it up as you normally would.

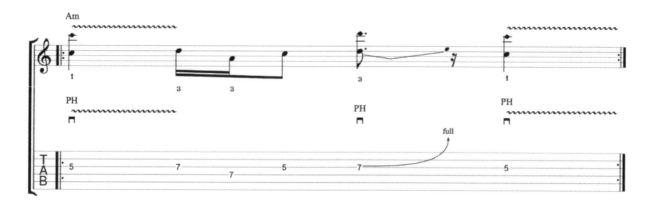

Now it's time for you to experiment with pinch harmonics. Try the following exercises:

1. Practice getting harmonics using up picks as well as down picks - experiment to find a way!
2. Try adding pinch harmonics to some of your favourite lick ideas
3. Experiment with using vibrato and bending with pinch harmonics
4. Try improvising over a backing track, working pinch harmonics into your solo

Have fun experimenting with this cool technique. Be patient too, it takes practice to be able to consistently produce pinch harmonics at will, it's not something most people *instantly* get the hang of. Keep refining and tweaking the technique and you'll eventually nail it. The solo study coming next gives you a few opportunities to practice your pinch harmonics too.

Solo Study: 'Deep Trouble'

Deep Trouble is an 8 bar rock solo in the key of D minor and uses string bending, vibrato, double stop bends, 16th note and sextuplet power moves, pinch harmonics and other devices we've seen so far in this book. It aims to give just *one* example of how some of the ideas we've studied can be combined into a short but effective rock solo.

I'll take you step-by-step through each of the licks in the solo and offer some helpful performance tips, but if you've worked thoroughly through the material so far then most of the solo will be self-explanatory.

Let's start by hearing how the solo sounds. Watch **Video 4.2 - Deep Trouble Solo Study** to see the solo demonstrated and get a feel for how it sounds (this video is part of your free bonus download pack, details in front of book). In the video I also show you each lick played up close at a slow tempo. Put this book down for a moment and watch **video 4.2** now.

Hopefully you love the solo and can't wait to play it - but first here are some important tips and considerations:

1. Each lick is 2 bars long, and they become progressively more challenging as you get further into the solo

2. I've made it super-easy to break the solo up into individual licks. Start by learning lick 1, practicing it until you can play it without difficulty. It doesn't need to be fast - but it does need to be **accurate**, **smooth**, and **in-time**

3. Next progress to lick 2. Get that to the same standard as lick 1, then practice joining them up to play bars 1-4 of the solo. Continue this process for licks 3 and 4 until you have the complete solo

4. Learn to sing the solo with your voice. This will really help you to nail the rhythm and timing

5. Pay attention to the spacing *between* the licks. Many people overlook this, resulting in a jumbled sounding performance. The timing between the licks is super-important - **get it right**!

6. Play it along with me in the video. Don't worry if you stumble or can't keep up to begin with - keep 'chasing' me and don't give up. This is one of the best ways to practice the solo, but don't attempt it until you think you're ready

7. When you're able to play *Deep Trouble* along with the video, try it on your own using the **backing track** provided. This may feel strange at first, keep going until you're happy with your performance

Ok let's break it down one lick at a time.

Lick 1 (Bars 1-2)

We start with a melodic bending lick. There's nothing too complicated here, but watch the rhythmic accuracy and tuning of the bends. Also remember to add vibrato to the string bend at the end of bar 1.

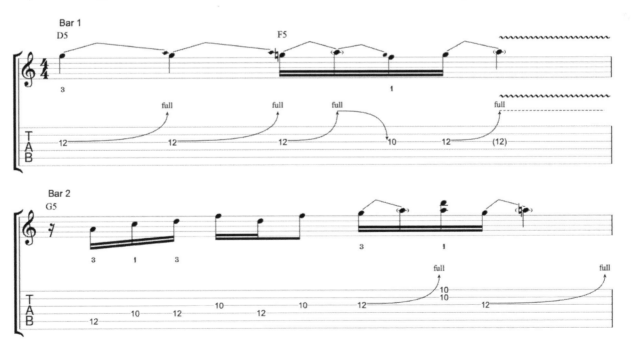

Lick 2 (Bars 3-4)

This lick should be pretty familiar, it's really just using some of the power moves from earlier in the book. It's great practice for your double-stop bends, I suggest you try out the fingering shown to help. The sextuplet phrase in bar 4 may test your speed and dexterity - slow it down and get it under control before you work on nailing it at the tempo I play it in the video. The picking directions show you the easiest way to pick this lick.

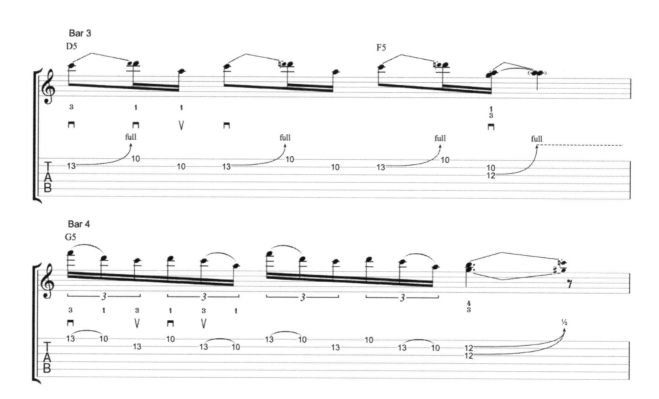

Lick 3 (Bars 5-6)

Bar 5 will put your bending technique to the test! Of course, aim to get this lick smooth and in-time with accurate bends before working it up to the target speed. In bar 6 we've got some pinch harmonics played in triplets down part of the D blues scale. I'm suggesting you use down picks for these, but change this if you wish. Don't forget the vibrato at the end of the lick - see if you can make that final pinch harmonic really scream!

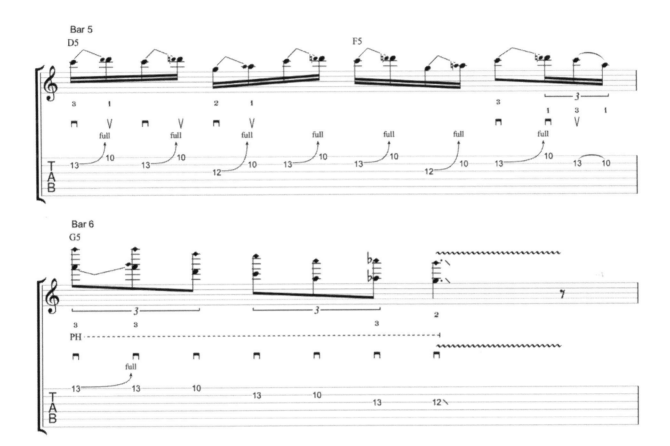

Lick 4 (Bars 7-8)

We close out with the most intense lick in the solo. Bar 7 repeats one of the power moves from earlier 3 times before ending on a high bend with added vibrato. You're going to want to break the more complex idea in bar 8 into small chunks - perhaps work on each beat in isolation before joining them together. A couple of specific things to notice are the pre-bend which starts the phrase and the 3rd finger slide before the final double-stop, make sure not to miss these. I suggest you use the fingering and picking guidelines for this lick, it will probably make it easier to play.

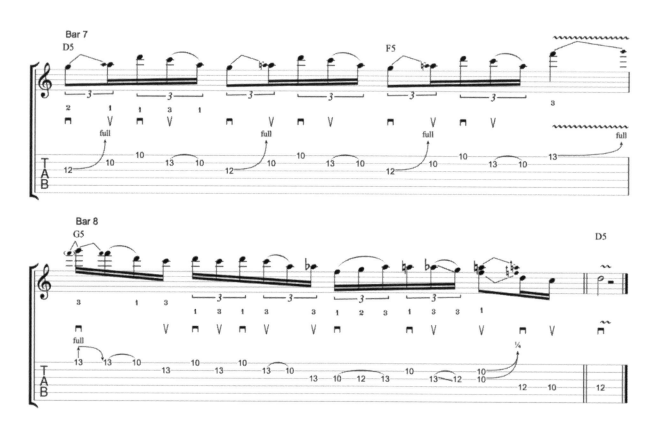

I hope you enjoy learning and playing *Deep Trouble*! Remember, take it steady, learning each lick individually before connecting them up to play the complete solo. I recommend that you *aim* to get it to the speed I play it, but don't worry if this doesn't happen overnight. The most important thing is that the licks are in time and accurately executed with a rock-solid rhythmic feel - this matters more than the speed you play it at, the ability to play the solo faster will come over time.

Final Thoughts on the *Deep Trouble* Solo

Deep Trouble displays a few musical qualities which we can take and use to play more effective solos. A few things to notice might be:

1. The licks tend to build in energy and intensity as the solo progresses (lick 1 is the slowest lick whereas lick 4 is the fastest)
2. The licks are using different rhythmic values to create contrast and interest. This is especially apparent in lick 3
3. Each lick has a clear and definite ending, one lick doesn't 'stumble' randomly into the next
4. The solo uses lots of repetition. This simple idea creates structure and logic - you don't need to play a brand-new idea on every beat of your solo!

Think about some of these concepts - how could you apply them to your own solos and improvisations?

Here's your Solo Challenge

Create your own solo based on *Deep Trouble*. You can keep/change as much of my solo as you want, just try to make sure you inject some of your own creativity and ideas into your new version. Also try to incorporate some of the concepts we just talked about when crafting your solo (using repetition, rhythmic diversity, contrast etc) - these are powerful principles and can have a massive influence on the impact your solos have. Above all, experiment and have fun. Good luck!

How To Boost Your Playing Speed

How Much Speed Do You Need?

The use of speed can be very effective in a solo - creating excitement, energy and contrast. It can also become very dull when *not* used in a musical way. We'll skip the pointless argument of whether playing fast beats playing slow and simply say this: playing fast is a creative tool, and it's how well we *use* speed which really matters.

The problem is that increasing playing speed can become addictive, and if we're not careful, it can end up being the main focus of our playing - a trap I have certainly fallen victim to at times. I think a balanced approach is needed - how much speed do **you** need to sound the way **you** want to sound? The answer to this question will change as your playing progresses and changes, but by asking yourself this you can work on developing the skills you actually *need*, rather than endlessly increasing your playing speed just for the sake of it!

With that said, if you've been struggling to play the licks in this book as fast as you want to - what can you do?

Building Speed with a Metronome

There are many approaches to building playing speed, but one of the most tried and tested methods involves using a metronome. Let's look at speeding up a power move using this approach (if you haven't got a metronome then look for an online one or browse your favourite app store, there are many free options).

Power moves are *perfect* exercises to use for building speed - they're short, they can easily be repeated and looped, and it's really easy to hear if you're staying in time as you play them. Even better, power moves represent much of what you'll probably *use* in your solos anyway, so the exercises you're practicing are directly linked to your playing.

The speed building method I'm about to show you could be applied to any power move, but for the purposes of this demonstration we'll use this one:

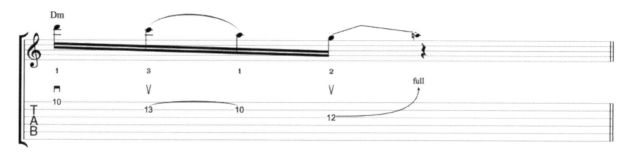

Step 1: Set the metronome to a slow setting. Choose what's right for you, but try 60-80 bpm (beats per minute) if you're not sure where to begin. Listen to the beat of the metronome for a moment to get a feel for it.

Step 2: Play the power move **once only** along with the click. Rest for a beat, then repeat. Practice this for a few minutes, taking short breaks as needed. The following diagram illustrates this approach:

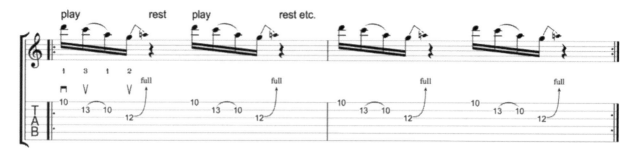

Step 3: Now, focus on your rhythm. Are you starting each repetition **right on the click**? Check you are, you shouldn't be starting the lick early or late! Also check the lick isn't slowing down and straying into the next beat.

I'm attempting to show this in the following diagram - the notes marked with * should be right on the click of the metronome:

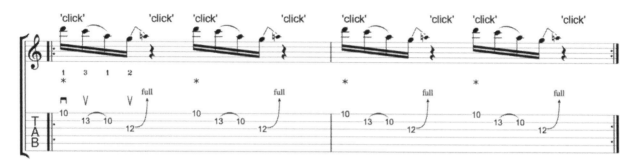

Step 4: When you're comfortable at your starting speed and the lick is totally in time, increase the speed of the metronome slightly (3-5 bpm) and **repeat** the exercise at the new speed.

Step 5: Keep ramping-up the speed of the click over time, steadily increasing the speed at which you can play the power move. Remember, never sacrifice timing and rhythmic accuracy for speed - fast and sloppy is **not** the goal!

This explanation should give you the general idea. You can of course adapt this exercise to achieve specific goals - for instance you might apply it to a longer lick, or even a complete solo. It's the *principle* behind this approach which is the important thing - use it to build whatever skills you're trying to develop.

Building Stamina

Building speed is one thing, but maintaining that speed for a length of time is slightly different - this is where building stamina comes in. The exercise can be easily adapted to build stamina as well as speed - simply repeat the lick more than once at a time, adding repetitions so that you're playing it for longer. The key is to add one repetition at a time so that you don't 'hit a wall' too soon! You might start with 2 repetitions followed by a rest as shown here. The click of the metronome is shown by the asterisk (*):

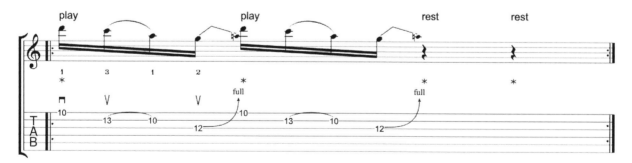

Then build up to 3 repetitions with a rest.

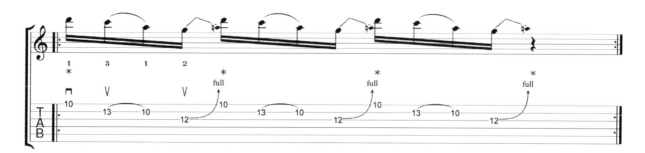

You get the idea: keep adding more and more repetitions to the exercise. Remember, get the timing rock-solid, don't let it become sloppy as you grow fatigued. If this happens then take a short break or play the lick fewer times.

If you work methodically with these exercises and you're sure to see the results you want. It probably won't happen overnight though, so be patient and consistent.

Try This!

Apply these metronome exercises to some power moves and licks from earlier chapters. You can also use them to build your speed on *Deep Trouble*. Don't be afraid to adapt and modify these approaches to make them work for you, there are dozens of powerful variations which you can apply. Good luck!

That's All For This Chapter

I hope you've enjoyed working through *Deep Trouble* and the other material we've examined here. We've covered some important principles in this chapter, so as always, take your time to work through it at a sensible pace - this way you can be confident that what you're learning will really make a difference to the kind of guitar player you're becoming.

Have fun, and when you're ready we'll build on what you've learned so far in the next chapter. See you then!

Ready To Move On?

- Can you play the *Deep Trouble* solo study?

- Are you confident with all the techniques used in the solo (bends, vibrato, pre-bends, pinch harmonics etc)?

- Have you learned some useful things from the solo study which you can apply to your own solos?

- Do you understand how to use a metronome to build your playing speed and fluency? Have you tried using these approaches?

- Do you feel confident with most of what we've studied in this book so far and are you ready for more?

If the answer to these questions is yes, and you genuinely feel like you're ready to move on then continue to the next chapter.

Chapter 5:
Repeating Licks, 'Sliding Scale' Runs and More

In this chapter we're going to expand your soloing vocabulary with repeating licks and 'sliding scale' patterns and runs. These topics are not only powerful soloing devices, they're also a lot of fun to play and experiment with. There's loads of cool stuff coming in this chapter, so grab your guitar and let's get started.

Repeating Licks

We've already seen some examples of repeating licks in this book, but now we're going to get into this topic in a bit more detail. In this lesson I'll show you some classic rock-style repeating licks you hear all the great players use, plus I'll show you how you can easily start to create repeating licks of your own.

Incidentally, if you enjoy this topic then you'll want to check out my in-depth book on repeating licks: **Repeating Rock Guitar Licks**. In that book I show you *hundreds* of repeating lick ideas you can use, plus give you a step-by-step method for building a library of killer repeating lick ideas. We also cover string-skipping, modal repeating licks, using stretches - and much more. This is a great way to master using this powerful rock and metal soloing tool!

What is a repeating lick?

Think of a **repeating lick** as a lick which is based on the repetition of a musical phrase. Put more simply, what we get when we play the same lick multiple times over. You might think this would sound boring, but actually the opposite is true: repeating licks can create energy, excitement, and tension in our solos - precisely why they're used so often by all the great rock and metal guitar players.

We used some repeating lick ideas in bar 5 and bar 7 of the Deep Trouble solo study from the previous chapter. Check them out in the following image - can you see the repetition happening?

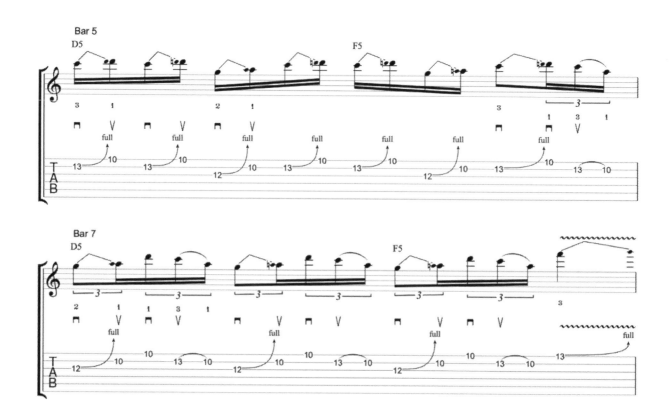

Try This Quick Exercise

Many of the blues-rock licks in chapters 2-3 could be described as repeating licks. Can you find them?

Classic Repeating Licks

Let's learn some of the repeating licks used by most leading rock players, this will help you get started using them in your solos. You'll probably recognise some of these from the playing of guitarists like Slash, Angus Young, Kirk Hammett, Zakk Wylde, Michael Schenker, Gary Moore, Steve Vai - in fact virtually all rock players have used these licks at some time!

As before, each lick has been given a star rating depending on how difficult it is. Picking and fingering guidelines are shown - I recommend following these, but change them if you want.

(**Important**: You can see each lick demonstrated at various speeds in **Video 5.1 Repeating Licks**. This is part of your **free downloadable bonus pack** - see the front of this book for details)

Lick 1 - Carbon Copy *

Our first repeating lick idea is simply the exact same thing played 3 times. The idea is then modified to create a strong ending. This might seem basic, but don't underestimate how effective this simple concept can be!

Here's your Lick Challenge

Transpose this lick into the keys of E minor, C minor A minor and G minor. Where possible, use the octave shift technique from earlier. Try using this example in a solo too, you may be surprised how great a simple lick like this can sound.

Lick 2 - Snakepit *

This simple-but-effective lick in the key of E minor is the kind of thing a player like Slash uses a lot. Hear how the momentum and energy build as you repeat the key phrase over and over? Also notice how the end of the lick uses a variation on the main phrase (the bend is simply moved to the neighbouring string). Enjoy!

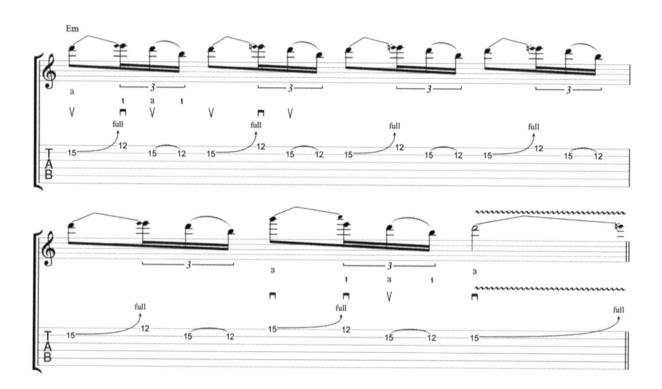

Here's your Lick Challenge

This lick mainly consists of the same phrase played over and over. Take this idea and use it to build a new repeating lick of your own. What happens if you repeat it less/more than in the example? Can you change the rhythm of the repeating phrase or modify it in some other way? Experiment to see what you can come up with, remembering to write out any cool licks you discover along the way.

Lick 3 - Down Under **

Here's a repeating lick I've heard Angus Young use. After repeating the same phrase 5 times in bar 1, we end with a Chuck Berry inspired idea in bar 2. Watch the rhythm on this lick - it's easy for it to unravel if you're not careful - slow it down and get it correct before you push the tempo.

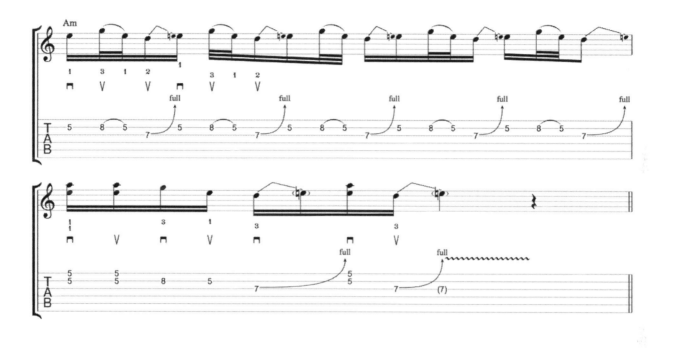

Here's your Lick Challenge

Can you create a new repeating lick using some of the ideas in bar 2 of *Down Under*? Experiment to see what you can come up with. Don't overcomplicate it - remember, simplicity can be powerful!

You may have noticed that most of these repeating licks are simply one or more of the power moves from earlier played multiple times. If you've spotted that for yourself then well done! Hopefully you can hear how this deceptively simple approach could be used to create an almost endless number of repeating licks to use in your solos? We're going to explore this in more depth in a moment, for now, see if you can spot some familiar power moves in the next batch of examples.

Lick 4 - Sea Dog ***

You often hear Jimmy Page use repeating licks in his ground-breaking style, and this example is a tribute to this timeless guitar legend. The lick is in the key of A minor and begins with a repeating blues-bending idea. In bar 2 we descend the A minor pentatonic scale using a common pattern or sequence, finishing the lick off with a simple unison bending move. Check out the fingering towards the end of bar 2 (highlighted with *) - using the 2nd and 3rd fingers as shown can make the string crossing move from the D string to the G string much easier, especially at quicker speeds.

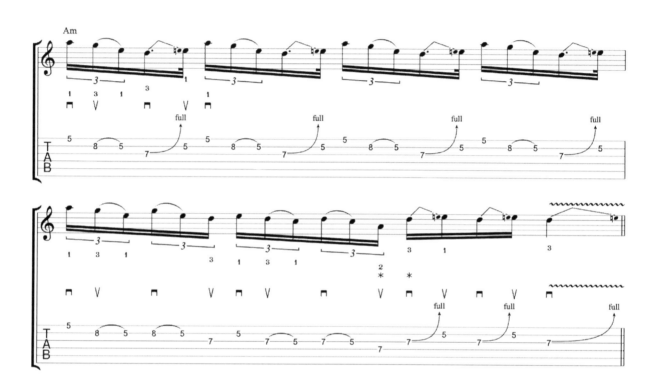

Here's your Lick Challenge

The bending idea in bar 1 is a common and powerful way to begin a repeating lick. Experiment with using this as the starting point for some repeating licks of your own. As I've said before, don't over complicate your licks - keep them simple, usable, and authentic - doing this will help them to stick in your vocabulary faster.

Lick 5 - Overtime ***

This Jimi Hendrix style lick is simply a 3 note phrase repeated over and over, but we're messing around with the rhythm to make things a little more interesting. In bar 1 the 3 note phrase is played as a rhythmic group of 3 - a triplet. Played like this, it fits neatly into each beat in the bar.

In bar 2 we change things a bit. The same phrase is played, but this time it is played in *16th note* rhythm. There are four 16th notes in a beat, but the phrase we're playing only lasts for *three* of them. This means that the phrase will begin again *before* the next beat instead of starting *on* it. This causes it to 'overlap' the beats, beginning in different places, instead of always starting on each beat. This is sometimes called rhythmic displacement and is a commonly used device in most music. Hopefully by analysing the example this will start to make sense, but the main thing is to recognise the resulting sound, and to experiment with using it in your own playing.

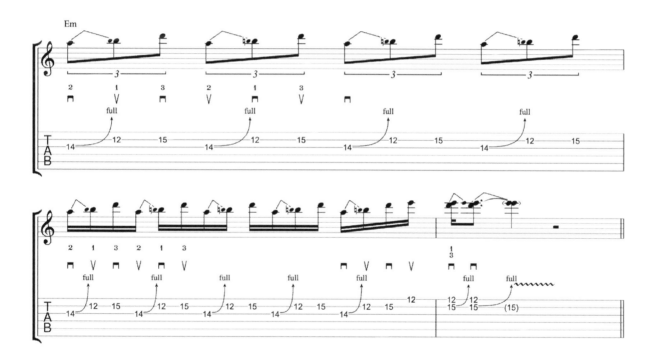

Here's your Lick Challenge

Practice the *Overtime* lick until you're really familiar with it. Then, practice playing the repeating phrase round and round, freely switching between rhythmic groups of 3 (triplets) and rhythmic groups of 4 (16th notes). This will help you to feel, hear, and ultimately use this rhythmic 'trick' instinctively in your solos. You can do this unaccompanied, but make sure to also try it over a drum groove or backing track to really hear the rhythmic effect it creates.

Lick 6 - Sledgehammer ***

Before we look at creating your own repeating licks, I've got one more example for you to play. This introduces a useful technique known as 'hammering on from nowhere'. This describes the practice of hammering *directly* onto a new string, the fretting hand playing the notes *without* any input from the picking hand.

The following exercise shows the difference between this technique and the more conventional way of playing. In the first bar we're picking each time we move to a new string. In the second bar only the first note in each phrase is picked - all the other notes are sounded with just the fretting hand. Try playing both versions to help you understand this idea.

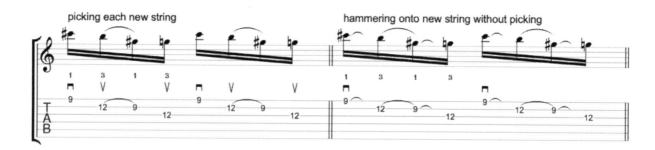

'Hammering on from nowhere' can be a very efficient way to play something because your picking hand doesn't need to do much - this can work especially well when you want to get something really fast. It will take practice to get it accurate, but it's definitely worth the effort.

The following example applies both approaches to the repeating C# blues scale idea we looked at a moment ago. We've also added an ending phrase to create a complete sounding lick. Follow the fingering for this example and make sure to try *both* ways of playing the repeating phrase to hear and feel the difference.

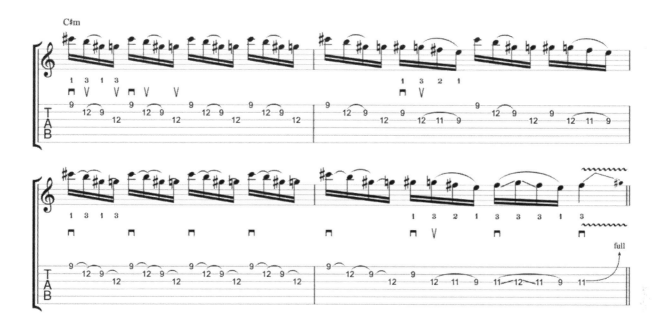

Here's your Lick Challenge

Practice inserting this repeating phrase into an improvisation over a backing track. Use a variety of different keys and focus on the 'hammering from nowhere' approach described. Also try to find other things to play with this technique, *many* common licks which use lots of hammer-ons and pull-offs can be played like this. Have fun!

Creating Your Own Repeating Licks

Notice how many of these examples are simply one or more power moves played multiple times? Well now it's your turn to experiment with this idea to see what you can learn and discover.

Take some of your favourite power moves and use them to build 5-6 repeating licks of your own.

A few tips to help you be successful with this:

1. Begin with just one power move in each lick
2. Consider repeating the power move 4-8 times to make the repetitive nature of the lick really clear
3. Make sure to 'wrap up' your licks with an ending phrase to make them sound complete, rather than unfinished
4. As you become more confident with this idea try combining more than one power move in a single lick
5. Practice your licks in a variety of keys

These tips are only here to help, they are **not** 'rules' so don't let them restrict you. If you want to disregard them entirely, then that's fine - being creative and finding some good licks which you like the sound of is all that matters here. So experiment, have fun, and remember to write out your best repeating lick ideas for future reference.

'Sliding Scale' Runs

So far in this book we've focused exclusively on using the 'shape 1' minor pentatonic and blues scale patterns in various keys. Getting a thorough grasp of these scales and building a large vocabulary of ideas based on them is *essential* in order to sound like an authentic rock or metal soloist, but now we're going to expand your scale knowledge a little with some *sliding* scale fingerings.

'Sliding' Scale Patterns

The 'shape 1' shapes we've seen so far stay in the same area of the fretboard and work *across* the strings. Sliding patterns help us to move *along* the fretboard as well. Doing this enables us to play different kinds of licks, reach some higher notes, and simply expand the range of things we can do on our guitar.

The following diagram shows the A minor pentatonic scale rearranged as a 'sliding' pattern. It is the same as the shape 1 pattern until it reaches the G string, where it begins to travel up the neck. The intervals are labelled for reference.

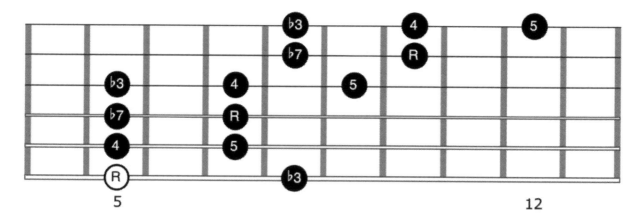

Fingerings for ascending and descending this scale pattern are shown in the following tab example. When using the scale to solo, other options may be preferable, but for playing up and down the scale pattern these work well.

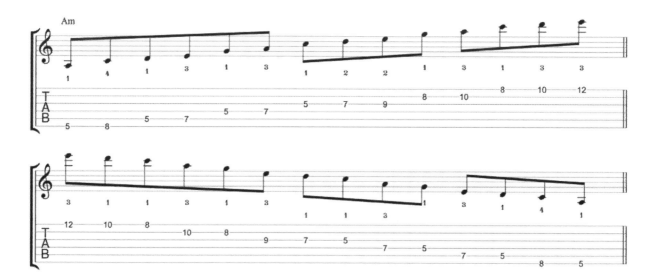

It is important to understand that the sliding and shape 1 scales are **exactly the same** thing because they contain the exact same *notes*. The sliding shapes are simply a way to *re-organise* these notes on the fretboard. The shape 1 and sliding scale patterns are **completely interchangeable** and sliding patterns can also be moved into other keys using the root note system discussed earlier.

By adding in the *b*5th interval, we can create a sliding blues scale pattern. This is shown in the following fretboard diagram. Use the tab example as a guideline for which fingers to use when ascending or descending the pattern - it's not the *only* fingering option, but I find it works well much of the time.

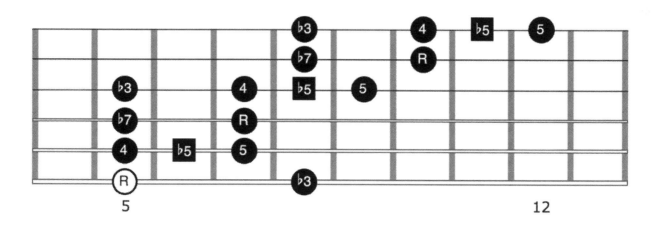

Now Test Yourself

Use the root note system explained earlier to play **sliding** minor pentatonic and blues scales in the following keys.

1. C minor
2. D minor pentatonic
3. E minor
4. G minor
5. F# minor

Getting Familiar with Sliding Scales

Hopefully you're now a much more confident soloist than you were when you started this book! For this reason, I'm going to let you become comfortable with these sliding scales on your own.

To do this:

1. Check you can seamlessly mix up the shape 1 and sliding patterns (they're almost the same anyway)
2. Come up with 5-10 power moves from the sliding patterns. Simply find some short ideas which you think sound good, write them out, and practice using them like you did with the power moves earlier in this book
3. Explore which notes at the top of the scale are good for string bending
4. Practice improvising using parts of the sliding scale. Experiment and jam, this will help you to discover how to use these patterns effectively

Good luck, and when you're ready we'll examine some sample licks - these will help you build your range of sliding scale ideas even more.

Sliding Scale Licks and Runs

The following licks will build your repertoire of versatile soloing ideas coming from the sliding scale patterns and help you learn to integrate them with the familiar shape 1 licks and power moves we looked at earlier in this book. As with previous licks, each example has a star rating indicating difficulty and suggested picking instructions are shown. Make sure to try out the fingerings for these licks, *especially* when position shifting to higher or lower frets using the sliding patterns - they'll help you find ways to seamlessly navigate around the fretboard (important!).

(**Note**: You can see each lick demonstrated at various speeds in **Video 5.2 Sliding Scale Licks**. This is part of your **free downloadable bonus pack** - see the front of this book for details)

Lick 1 - Zepwire *

This Jimmy Page style lick is in the key of A minor and introduces a simple way to combine the shape 1 and sliding minor pentatonic scales. Pay special attention to what's happening in bar 2 - it gives you some valuable ideas to use for creating your own sliding scale licks.

Here's your Lick Challenge

To get you used to playing sliding scale licks in all keys, transpose this lick into the keys of E minor, C minor, G minor and C# minor. Also try it out over some suitable backing tracks to help consolidate it into your vocabulary.

Lick 2 - Down With Joe *

This blues based lick is the kind of thing someone like Joe Perry would play, and it presents you with lots of sliding scale ideas. Bar 1 shows you how to shift into the sliding pattern by sliding along the B string - make sure to get comfortable with this move, it's very useful. In bars 2-3 we see some of the best sounding string bends in the sliding scale shape including a 3 fret bend on the top E string (push!). Make sure to memorise where all these bends are, they'll really help you learn to use the sliding scale shape in a musical way. Also notice the cool idea in the second half of bar 2 when we descend the A blues scale down the top E string. There's enough in this lick to keep you busy for a while - enjoy!

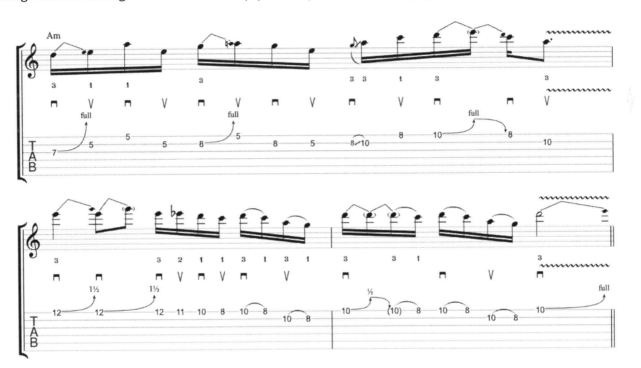

Here's your Lick Challenge

Harvest this lick for some cool sliding scale power moves. Pay special attention to the bits of the lick I mention in the description, as well as stealing anything else you think will be useful. Then practice using these power moves over backing tracks to ingrain them into your playing vocabulary. If you want to be really thorough, do all this in multiple keys too.

Lick 3 - Rocky Road **

This lick will help you get comfortable with 'jumping' from shape 1 straight up to the top part of the sliding scale pattern. Practice this lick until you can do this easily - it will help you learn to combine all these scale patterns into an awesome sounding rock guitar style.

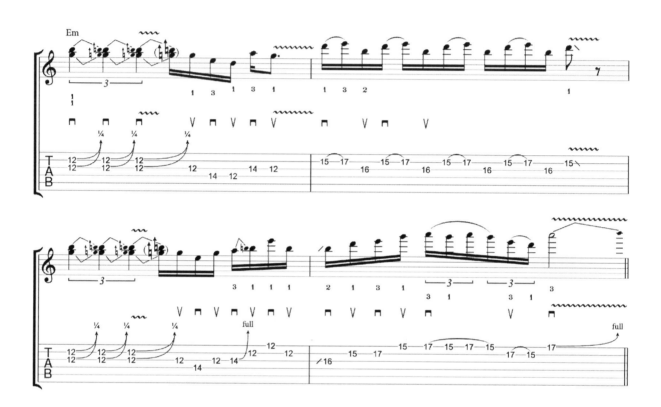

Here's your Lick Challenge

Using my example as a guideline, can you make up 2-3 of your own licks which 'jump' between shape 1 and the sliding pattern? Write out your best licks so you can explore them later.

Also practice improvising over a jamtrack, *forcing* yourself to keep switching between both scale shapes to focus your attention on building this skill, rather than slipping back into your comfort-zone and playing all the things you'd normally play. Work in all areas of the scale, especially the bits that don't feel so comfortable - then soon you'll be able to fluently jump between these patterns with ease. Practice this exercise in different keys too.

Lick 4 - Going Nowhere **

This repeating lick in C minor shows how you can move a simple pull-off phrase from shape 1 into the sliding pattern. I'm playing this using the 'hammering from nowhere' technique we talked about earlier - feel free to pick it some more if you prefer. Check out those useful bends in bars 2-3 as well.

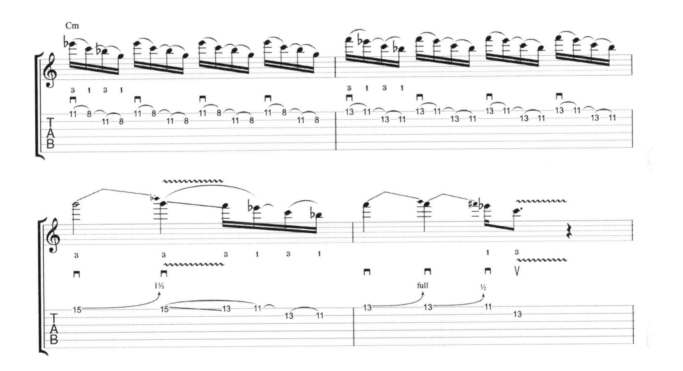

Here's your Lick Challenge

Can you find some other pull-off/hammer-on phrases which you can easily move between the two scale patterns? See if you can make them work over a backing track and keep a record of your best ideas. See if you can improvise some 'on the spot' as well.

'Tweaking' the Sliding Scale Pattern for Repeating Octaves

We'll see some more sliding scale licks in a moment, but first, I want to show you a cool trick you can do to the sliding scale fingering. First, we'll move the b3rd from the low E string onto the A string. Then we'll add the b7th onto the low E string as well. Study the following diagram to see this happening - notice how the rest of the scale is the same as before, it's only the low E and A string which have changed.

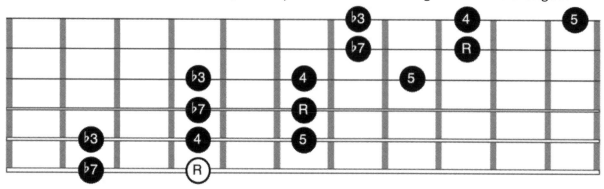

We can also add the b5th interval to get a blues scale fingering.

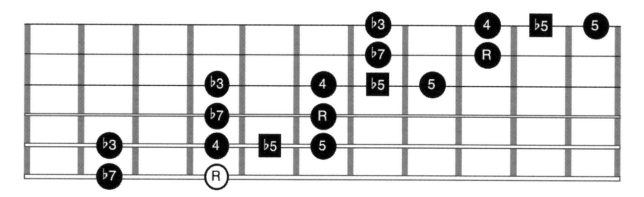

These alternative scale patterns simply give you more options when it comes to soloing. Personally, I prefer this fingering for the scale, I find it easier to use and like the fact that it goes down to a lower note than the other one (the b7th we just added).

Another cool thing about these patterns is the symmetry they contain: the exact same fingering pattern is duplicated in 3 octaves. How this applies to the blues scale shape is shown in the following images. To see how this works in the minor pentatonic scale simply take the b5th out.

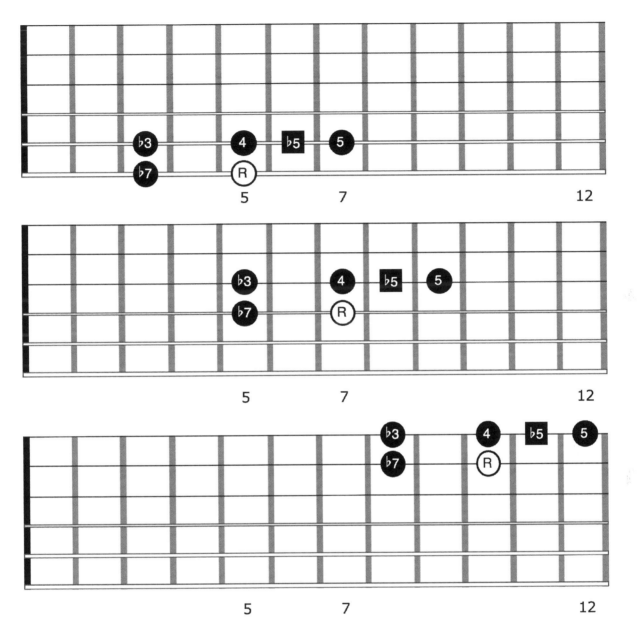

Play through this pattern in all three octaves to help this concept make sense - we'll be seeing how it can be used in some of the licks coming shortly.

Now Test Yourself

Practice playing the modified fingerings for the minor pentatonic and blues scales in the following keys. As you do, pay special attention to the way the same pattern duplicates across 3 octaves.

1. G minor
2. A minor pentatonic
3. C# minor
4. D minor
5. F# minor

Lick 5 - Steppin' Up **

This lick will help you become familiar with the repeating octaves inside our modified sliding pentatonic pattern. We're basically repeating the same idea through 3 octaves, finishing with a speedy descending blues scale run. I'm using 'hammering from nowhere' to play the final part of the example but feel free to play it differently if you prefer. Also, pay attention to the fingering given for the position shifts, it'll help you get them accurate.

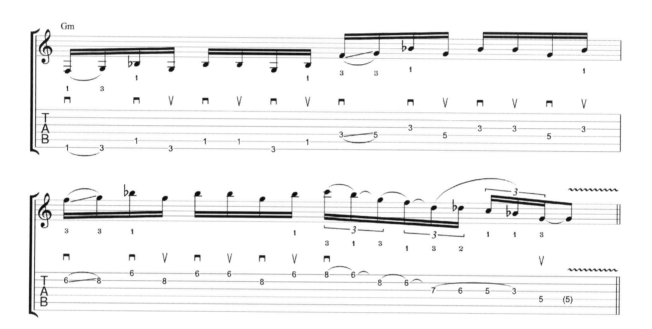

Here's your Lick Challenge

Find some simple patterns similar to the one being used here and practice duplicating them in 3 octaves as in the *Steppin' Up* lick. You could also try starting at the *top* of the pattern and moving *down* in octaves instead of going up. Finally, practice playing *Steppin' Up* one octave higher by moving it up above the 12th fret.

Lick 6 - Satch-O-Slider ***

This lick is moving up through the B blues scale pattern using *legato* technique. This is the name used to describe combining fretting hand techniques like hammer-ons, pull-offs and slides to create smooth, fluid sounding lines. *Satch-O-Slider* isn't that difficult, but follow the fingering to help you execute the position shifts and get it up to speed. Also make sure to get the timing under control - it's easy to drift out of time with licks like this. By the way, you may like to add the little blues scale flurry on the top 2 strings in the second bar to your collection of power moves?

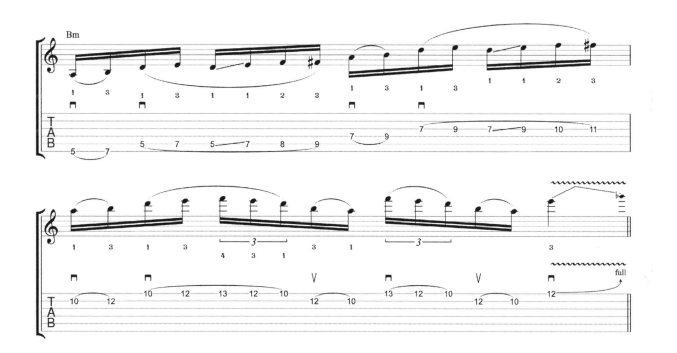

Here's your Lick Challenge

This lick is perfect for practicing your fretting hand technique and accuracy. It's also a great way to fine-tune your position shifting technique as you ascend this scale pattern. Move it into at least 6 other keys to help you nail this skill in different areas of the fretboard.

Lick 7 - Scary's Blues ***

In this example we're taking a repeating blues scale idea down through the sliding A blues scale. Although this lick is fast, the fingering and shape is exactly the same in each octave - making it easier to get the complete lick happening. This lick is a great chop building exercise for your fretting hand and will help you build finger independence, speed, accuracy and control. Also, try to play the final phrase using 'hammering from nowhere' as shown in the tablature. This lick is kind of challenging, so break it up into convenient fragments and work slowly on these before trying to string them together to play the entire lick. The suggested fingering is economical and efficient so give it a try. Good luck!

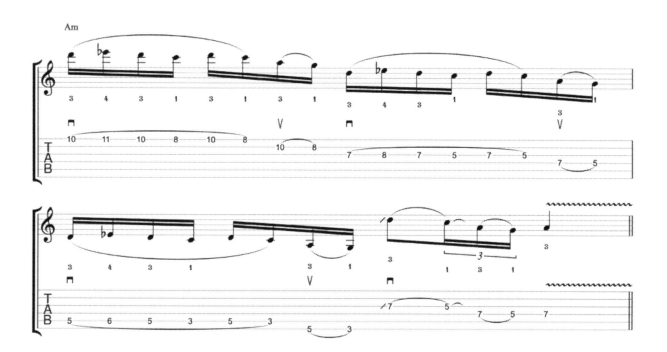

Here's your Lick Challenge

The repeating blues scale idea making up this lick is 2 beats long, and is a great addition to your soloing vocabulary. It can be used in many different ways to create some really cool sounds. See if you can create some licks of your own using this idea. You can play it in one octave, or move it into different octaves as shown in the example - it's up to you. Perhaps you could try going up the scale playing this fragment? Try all sorts of possibilities, I think you'll find that you discover some great soloing ideas. Enjoy!

Lick 8 - Blue and Confused ***

We'll close this chapter with a whirlwind tour through the sliding and shape 1 A blues scale patterns. I strongly suggest that you follow the fingering shown for this lick, there are a lot of position shifts to negotiate and a bullet-proof fingering strategy will be a big help. Break the lick up into small parts to learn and practice it, then reconnect the pieces when you feel ready. As always, keep everything slow, controlled and in-time - this really is important. In the final bar we're playing 4 notes along the top E string using a stretch instead of a position shift - follow the fingering shown for a great fretting hand exercise.

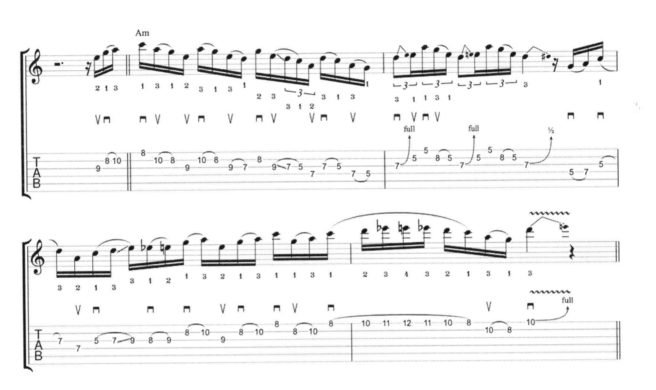

Here's your Lick Challenge

There is a lot happening in this lick! Break it up into small, manageable chunks which you can commit to memory, then practice using these in some solos and licks of your own. You'll find the parts of this lick very valuable in building cool licks which employ shape 1 and sliding scale patterns. Make sure to explore some different keys too.

That's All For This Chapter

I hope you've found chapter 5 fun, informative, and that it's helping you to discover all sorts of new possibilities and ideas to use in your playing. Like I say at the end of every chapter - there is no rush. It's super-important to give yourself time to explore and experiment with new material in an unhurried way, so don't put pressure on yourself to move on before you feel ready. Take your time, play around with new ideas, and just enjoy the journey - in my experience we actually progress faster this way which is of course an added bonus!

Remember, if you've enjoyed the repeating licks section of this chapter and want to go deeper into this exciting area of rock guitar playing, then check out my **Repeating Rock Guitar Licks** method book to learn everything you'll probably ever need to know.

Good luck with this chapter, have fun, and when you're ready I'll see you in the next chapter.

Ready To Move On?

- Can you play some of the repeating lick examples and have you practiced working them into your solos?

- Have you created some cool repeating licks of your own? Have you practiced using these?

- Do you understand, know how to play, and practiced using all the sliding scale patterns in this chapter?

- Can you play the sliding scale lick examples and created some sliding licks of your own using the tips and exercises provided?

- Do you feel like this chapter has boosted your playing skills and soloing vocabulary?

If the answer to these questions is yes, then when you're ready, continue to the next chapter.

Chapter 6:
Major Pentatonic Rock Soloing

So far we've focused exclusively on playing in minor keys using tools like the minor pentatonic scale. As a rock guitarist you'll be playing in minor keys much of the time, but this will not *always* be the case, and to be a versatile rock guitarist you also need to be able to play in a major key.

In this chapter I'm going to show you how to adapt most of what we've studied so far to play rock solos in major keys. Let's get into it.

The Major Pentatonic Scale

The major pentatonic scale is what most rock guitarists use when they need to solo in a major key. There are other options too, but this approach is the best place to begin.

To learn all about the major pentatonic scale, see **Volume 1** of my **Music Theory for Guitarists** series. We'll briefly recap on the basics now, but I want to avoid getting *too* bogged down in the theory and focus on practical applications and examples. We do need to cover *some* theory though, so read on...

What Is the major pentatonic scale?

The major pentatonic scale is a 5 note scale. It's interval formula is:

Root + 2nd + 3rd + 5th + 6th

You can also think of it as the major scale with the 4th and 7th notes removed:

C major scale: C D E F G A B

C major pentatonic: C D E G A

By leaving F (4th) and B (7th) out of the C major scale we get the C major pentatonic scale. This gives a 'stripped down' version of the major scale which works great for playing in major keys.

How is the major pentatonic used?

In most cases a straightforward approach works the best: simply play the major pentatonic scale which goes with the key you're soloing in. When soloing in A major, use the A major pentatonic scale. If soloing in E major, use the E major pentatonic scale and so on.

Can you use the minor pentatonic scale in a major key?

In theory, this would sound wrong - but in practice it *can* sometimes sound great when done skilfully. Rock players often mix the sound of major and minor pentatonics together to get a major sound with a cool, blues edge. We'll be getting into this later in this chapter.

That's all on the major pentatonic scale theory for now. Remember to see **Volume 1** of my **Music Theory for Guitarists** series to learn more about major keys and the major pentatonic.

Turning Minor Pentatonic Scales into Major Pentatonics

The easiest way to get up and running with the major pentatonic scale is to take the minor pentatonic patterns we saw in the previous chapters and *convert* them into major pentatonics. This is easier than it sounds: you simply need to move them **down 3 frets**.

For example, 'shape 1' A minor pentatonic at the 5th fret (top diagram) becomes A *major* pentatonic when we move it down 3 frets to the 2nd fret (bottom diagram). Notice how the intervals in the diagrams change to reflect the interval formula of the major pentatonic scale (Root, 2, 3, 5, 6).

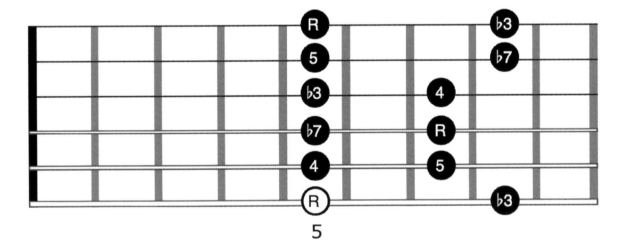

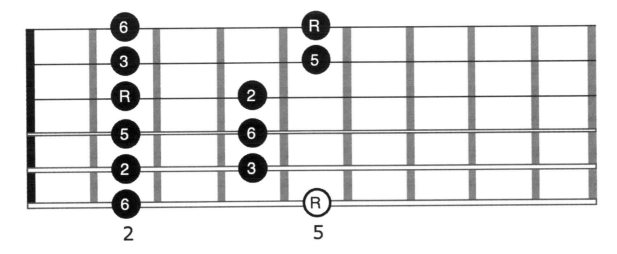

We can also move the sliding pattern down 3 frets to get a useful sliding major pentatonic shape:

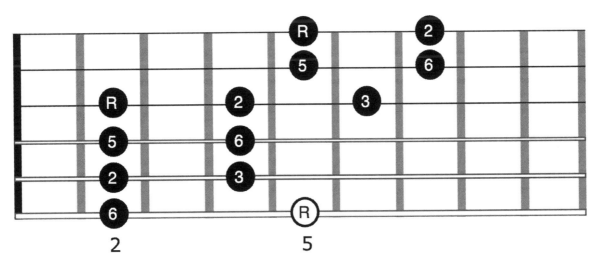

This 'trick' is all to do with **relative major** and **relative minor** keys. Every major key has a relative minor key. The major and minor pentatonics for each of these related keys contain the *exact* same notes. Look at the bottom diagram from a moment ago again - see how the A major pentatonic pattern at the 2nd fret is also F# minor pentatonic? This is because F# minor is the relative minor key of A major - the same pattern can be used to play either scale. For more information on relative major and minor keys see **Volume 1** of my **Music Theory for Guitarists** series.

Try This Quick Exercise

Let's practice converting minor pentatonics into major pentatonic scales now. Use shape 1 and the sliding patterns to play the following major pentatonic scales. For some keys you may need to go above the 12th fret. Check yourself with the answers that follow.

1. C major pentatonic
2. E major pentatonic
3. D major pentatonic

4.   G major pentatonic
5.   F major pentatonic
6.   C# major pentatonic

(**Answers**: You should be playing shape 1 at the following frets: (1) 5th fret (2) 9th fret (3) 7th fret (4) 12th fret (5) 10th fret (6) 6th fret).

Recycle Your Minor Pentatonic Licks!

We've just seen how minor pentatonic scale patterns become major pentatonic scales when we move them down 3 frets.

This means that any minor pentatonic licks you know can become major pentatonic licks, simply by shifting them down 3 frets too!

Whilst this approach is very useful, you do need to experiment to get really good at using it, and the most incredible minor pentatonic lick won't *necessarily* sound as good when used in a major pentatonic setting. Handle this short-cut with a bit of care, but with practice and experience you'll become attuned to the sound of the major pentatonic scale and you'll find yourself intuitively making good choices about what to play.

Try This Quick Exercise

Choose a minor key you feel comfortable playing in. Now, move your favourite lick ideas down 3 frets to turn them into major pentatonic licks. Compare the difference in sound to help you become familiar with the different flavours the two scales give.

Now, find a backing track in the major key you are using and practice jamming with your 'recycled' licks, using them to play some cool major key solo ideas. Have fun...

Major Pentatonic Power Moves

The following selection of power moves will help to kickstart your major pentatonic soloing. Some of these are very similar to the minor pentatonic power moves from earlier, but they also work great in a major pentatonic context.

All these power moves feature at least one string bend. Make sure to execute the right *kind* of bend - you'll find pre-bends, double-stop bends and other bending approaches in these. I've left the picking up to you, but suggested fingerings are given where I think they will be helpful. All of these examples are shown in the key of D major - practice transposing them to other keys as well.

Note: all these power moves are demonstrated in **Video 6.1 - Major Pentatonic Power Moves,** available in your free bonus download pack (see front of book for details).

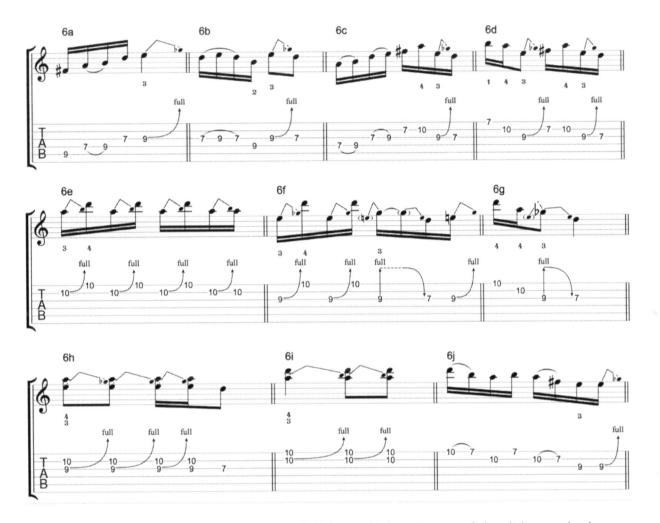

The following power moves show you some useful ideas which make use of the sliding scale shape.

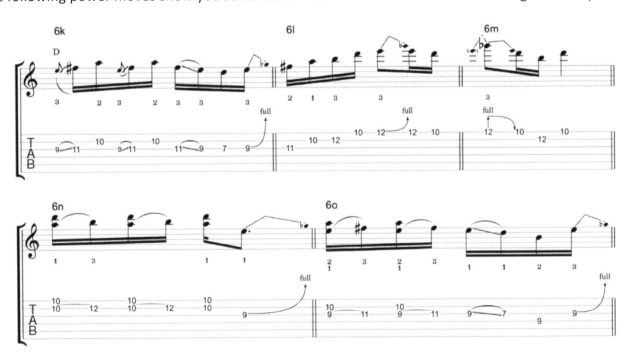

Try This Quick Exercise

Find a backing track in the key of D major and try out these power move ideas. Playing each one *over and over* the backing will help to become really familiar with it. Invest some time into this, it will make a *big* difference to your grasp of major pentatonic soloing as well as help you work through the rest of this chapter.

When you're ready, try working the power moves into some improvised solos over the backing track. Of course, you eventually want to do all of these things in some other keys as well.

'Major Daze' Solo Study

Now we'll look at how to combine some of our major pentatonic ideas to create a melodic rock solo. *Major Daze* is a ballad style solo study in the key of E major, and makes extensive use of many of the power move ideas we've seen so far in this chapter.

Before we begin watch **Video 6.2 - Major Daze Solo Study** to hear the solo and see each lick played at a slow tempo. After that I'll take you step-by-step through each lick in the solo. Remember to apply all the guidelines and tips I gave you for learning the *Deep Trouble* solo study from earlier, and when you're ready, practice the solo over the **Major Daze backing track**.

Lick 1 (Bars 1-2)

This lick uses common major pentatonic bending moves to give the solo a strong, melodic beginning. Aim to get the tuning on the bends accurate and make sure to get the rhythm solid with this lick - it's easy to rush long notes like we're seeing here. You may find the fingering suggestions useful so check them out too.

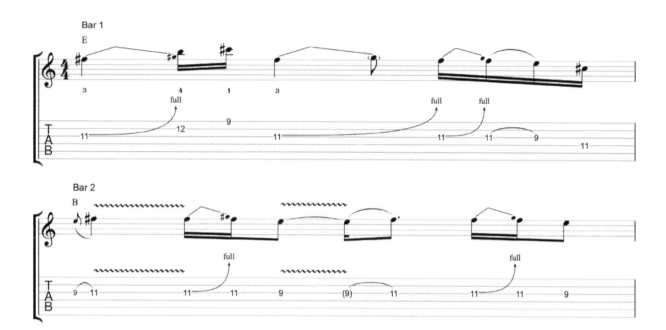

Lick 2 (Bars 3-4)

In bar 3 you can see a common minor pentatonic idea being employed in a major pentatonic context to give a sudden 'burst' of speed. This contrasts nicely with the long bends at the start of the bar. In bar 4 we end the lick with a tasty sliding phrase - follow the fingering here to ensure you don't skip the slide.

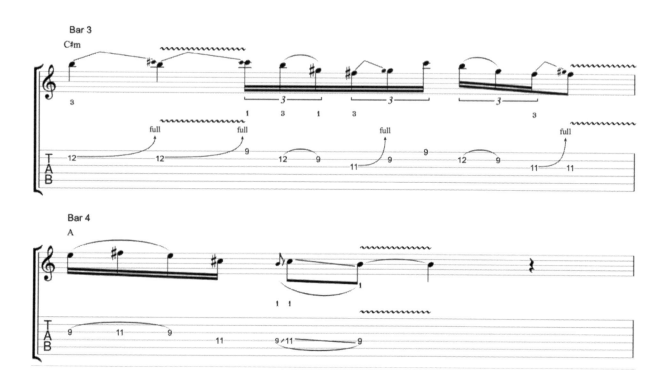

Lick 3 (Bars 5-6)

Check out the cool double stop hammer-on moves that begin lick 3 - they're a really tasty addition to your soloing vocabulary. Halfway through bar 5 we begin to work our way up the sliding scale shape to access some melodic bends and pre-bends at the top of the scale. Follow the fingering given to make it easier to negotiate the position shift smoothly.

Lick 4 (Bars 7-8)

In bar 6 we continue with the bending ideas seen in bar 5. This creates a strong sense of continuity between the two licks because they're using some of the same melodic material. Finally in bar 8 we close the solo with a rapid pentatonic idea which may remind you of Eric Johnson's playing. This isn't that hard to play, but it will probably take you some time to work this lick up to speed. Of course, work on it in smaller chunks and get the timing under control before focusing on getting the lick up to performance speed. I strongly suggest you follow the picking and fingering guidelines given - they'll almost certainly make this lick easier to play.

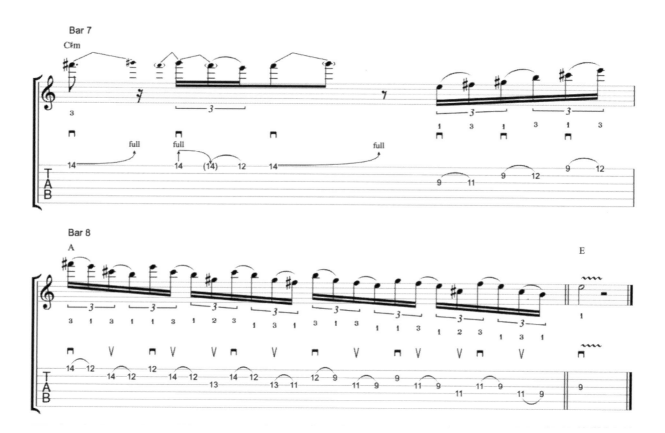

Some Final Thoughts on *Major Daze*

As well as learning lick ideas from this study, *Major Daze* can give you some ideas about how to structure an effective solo. Check out the following ideas.

1. The licks build in energy and intensity as the solo progresses (lick 1 is the slowest lick whereas lick 4 is the fastest)

2. As the solo progresses we're working up to the higher notes and bends. This helps the solo to 'build' and sound like it's going somewhere, stopping it from stagnating

3. We're not staying in one rhythmic 'gear' for very long. This creates rhythmic contrast and gives the solo forward momentum

Can you spot these concepts at work in the solo? Try to employ them in your own solos - they can make a big difference.

Try These Practice Tasks

1. Create a solo of your own over the **Major Daze backing track**. Get creative with what the solo study has taught you, experiment, and have fun working on your major pentatonic soloing skills

2. Find some backing tracks online in a selection of different major keys (there are thousands on YouTube for example). Practice jamming over them applying some of what you learned from studying the power moves and the *Major Daze* solo. Experiment, try things out, make mistakes - this is how you'll become comfortable soloing in any major key. Have fun!

Mixing Minor and Major Pentatonics

When soloing in a minor key it's best to stick to minor scales like the minor pentatonic and blues scale. Playing the major pentatonic is not a good idea in this setting.

When soloing in a major key however, it's possible to sneak in some minor pentatonic scale and blues scales ideas alongside our major sounds. This adds a darker, bluesy edge to our licks and solos, and acts as a powerful contrast to the 'sweeter' sound of the major pentatonic.

We have to be careful when using this approach, it can go *badly* wrong! As a guideline, think of playing major pentatonic most of the time, dipping into the minor pentatonic and blues scales for some different flavour. As with everything in this book, experimentation and trial-and-error is how you'll learn to do this, but let's look at a few ways you can get started.

Shifting Scale Patterns and *Split Shift* Solo Study

Perhaps the easiest method for mixing major and minor pentatonic sounds is to simply shift the same scale pattern around by 3 fret intervals at certain places in your solo. The following short solo example, *Split Shift*, is in the key of A major and demonstrates some easy ways to get to grips with this approach. The tab has some fingering suggestions, but mostly I've left it up to you to decide the best way to play it. Make sure to analyse where we're shifting between major and minor scales too and when you're ready practice playing the solo over the designated **backing track**. Watch **Video 6.3 Split Shift Solo Study** to see and hear this solo being demonstrated.

Split Shift

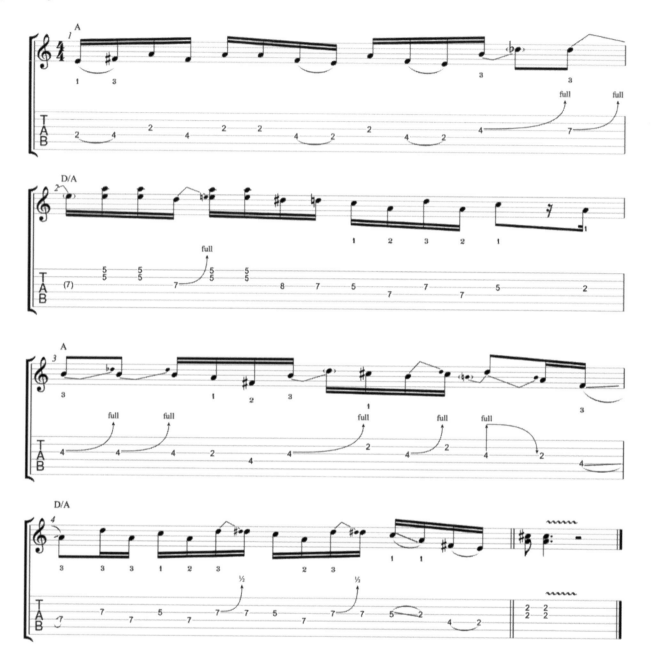

Try These Practice Tasks

1. Practice improvising over the **Split Shift backing track,** switching between major and minor sounds. Persevere if you can't get it to work at first - with practice you'll get it sounding better

2. Create a short solo of your own which uses this approach. Base your solo around *Split Shift* or create something entirely new, it's your choice

3. Find some backing tracks in other major keys and practice using this 'switching' method over them to mix up major and minor scale sounds

The 'Blues Scale Hack' and *Countryman* Solo Study

We know minor pentatonic scale patterns can be moved down 3 frets to get major pentatonic shapes. When we do the same thing with the *blues scale* something interesting happens: the *b*5th interval in the blues scale becomes the *b*3rd of the relative major pentatonic scale. The result, a major pentatonic scale with an added *b*3rd. This is shown in the following diagram with the *b*3rd notes shown as white squares:

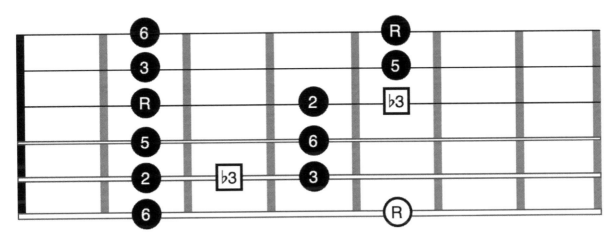

This gives us an easy way to work some minor pentatonic flavour into our major pentatonic soloing, and it's a fantastic way to spice up those major pentatonic licks without needing to physically move the scale shape around. Check out the top country and country-rock players to hear this approach used a lot.

One of the most common devices you'll hear is the movement from the minor 3rd to the major 3rd (*b*3rd to 3rd). The following short licks will familiarise you with this idea before we see it used in the *Countryman* solo study coming in a moment. The following examples are shown in the key of D with minor to major 3rd moves highlighted by an asterisk (*).

Now we'll put some of these ideas together into a complete solo. *Countryman* is a country-rock style solo in the key of D major and makes extensive use of the major pentatonic with the added *b*3rd. Watch **Video 6.4 - Countryman Solo Study** to hear the solo and see each lick played at a slow tempo, then work through the solo one lick at-a-time. I've included fingering guidelines where I think it might be helpful but feel free to alter these. When you can play the solo, practice playing it along with the **Countryman backing track**.

Countryman

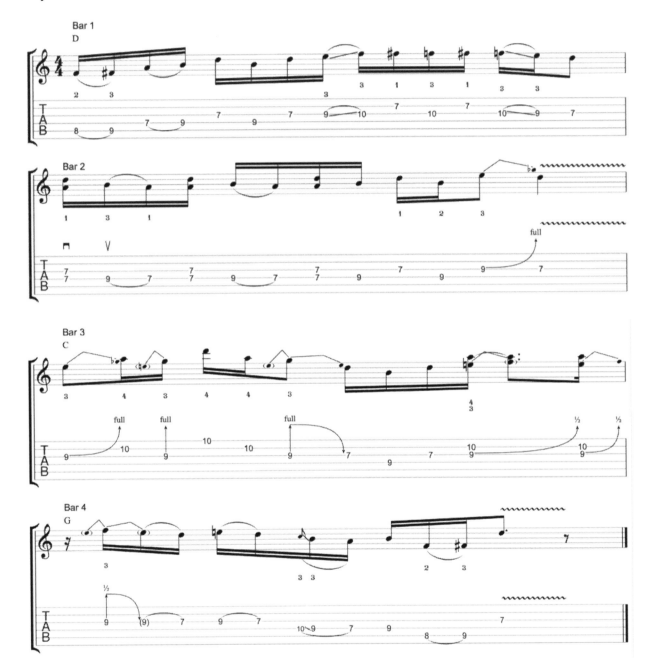

Performance Tips

By now you should be pretty confident working through a study like this on your own, but I want to discuss a few important things about this solo to help you get the most from learning it.

1.   The licks are predominantly derived from the D major pentatonic scale. This is in keeping with the major key tonality of the solo. The *b*3rd is just added in places for effect

2.   We can play the *b*3rd by bending the 2nd up a semitone (semitone bend on the G string, 9th fret). Remember this cool device for your major key soloing vocabulary!

3.   In bar 4 we're executing a quick slide down from the 10th fret on the D string. This note is found in the D minor pentatonic scale too - maybe experiment with using it over the backing track?

Try These Practice Tasks

Create a solo of your own over the **Countryman backing track**. Try using some of the *Countryman* licks and ideas in your solo - this will help them stick in your memory and your playing. Also practice improvising over the backing track, trying out some of what the study has taught you.

That's All For This Chapter

I hope you've enjoyed learning major key soloing and the major pentatonic scale.

We could go *much* deeper into this topic, discussing all sorts of other ideas - but the approaches I've shown you are what rock players seem to use most of the time. Practicing and becoming comfortable using these will enable you to fire out authentic rock solos over almost any rock style song in a major key! If you want to learn more about the major pentatonic scale and how to use it then see my **CAGED System for Guitar** book to learn all the major pentatonic scale shapes plus loads more sample licks to play.

Work through this chapter at your own pace and when you're ready I'll see you in the next chapter where we're going to go beyond pentatonic sounds by looking at the natural minor scale and Dorian modes.

Ready To Move On?

- Are you comfortable using minor pentatonic shapes to play major pentatonic scales in any key?

- Have you learned and practiced applying the major pentatonic power moves?

- Have you studied and played the *Major Daze* solo study?

- Do you understand how to mix up major and minor pentatonic sounds?

- Can you play *Split-Shift* and *Countryman*? Have you practiced applying the concepts we see being used in these solo studies?

If the answer to these questions is yes, then when you're ready, continue to the next chapter!

Chapter 7:
Going Beyond Pentatonics with Natural Minor and Dorian Sounds

Until now this book has focused only on pentatonic and blues scales. This makes perfect sense simply because the *vast* majority of rock guitar vocabulary uses these scales. In fact, I'd suggest it's almost *impossible* to sound like an authentic rock soloist *without* developing a solid pentatonic, blues based vocabulary. Add to this the fact that your pentatonic vocabulary will actually *help* you learn to use other common rock scales - and you can hopefully see why pentatonic and blues scales are so important!

But when you are ready to explore some new scales and sounds used by rock and metal guitarists, the best place to begin is by learning about the **natural minor scale** (or **Aeolian mode**) and **Dorian mode**. We're going to dive into these scales now.

The Natural Minor Scale

The natural minor scale is simply a minor pentatonic with two additional notes: the **2nd** (or **9th**) and the **b6th** intervals. It works great when playing in many minor key situations and is used extensively by rock guitarists. You'll also hear the natural minor scale being called the **Aeolian mode**, this is simply an alternative name for the same thing.

I'm not going to go into *all* the theory relating to the natural minor scale here because it's a topic I've covered in some of my other books. Instead, I want to concentrate on getting you started with *using* it effectively in your playing. We'll cover some basics, but for detailed information on the natural minor scale, what it is, and when to use it see my **Music Theory for Guitarists** series.

The following diagram shows you the most common way to play the natural minor scale. Notice how it is built around our shape 1 minor pentatonic scale pattern (shown by the black circles in the diagram). We'll look at why this is important in a moment, for now take a moment to learn the pattern.

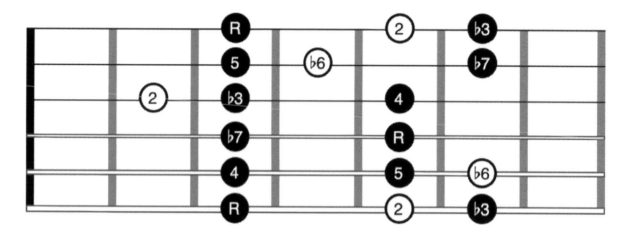

When do you use the natural minor scale?

You can try using the natural minor scale anytime when you might use the minor pentatonic. To be clear, I'm not saying it will *always* work - but in many minor key situations it will. We know that the minor pentatonic scale normally works great for minor key soloing, and this makes up most of the natural minor scale anyway. The 2nd or 9th is a versatile interval which will normally sound good when combined with the minor pentatonic. The *b*6th interval is the note which *sometimes* may sound like it doesn't fit, so this is the note to watch. If it does sound ok in your solo, then chances are the natural minor scale is a good fit for the chords you're playing over.

The Minor Pentatonic Framework and the *b*5th Interval

The natural minor shape is built around the shape 1 minor pentatonic pattern, and we can use this to our advantage. Instead of trying to build a whole *new* vocabulary around the natural minor scale, simply *decorate* your minor pentatonic ideas by adding in the 2nd and *b*6th intervals. It makes no sense to discard all the minor pentatonic material you've taken the time to learn - you can use it to quickly become fluent with natural minor soloing too! Look for this at work in the examples which are coming shortly.

A cool way to add some bluesy tension to the natural minor scale is to *add* the *b*5th interval from the blues scale. You can see this in the following diagram, the *b*5th is shown as white square.

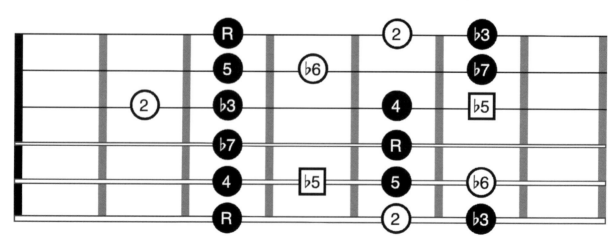

This gives us a collection of notes we can use and combine to create some cool sounding soloing ideas. We'll look at some examples next, but first try the following exercise.

Try This Quick Exercise

1.   Play shape 1 minor pentatonic anywhere on the fretboard
2.   Add the 2nd to the pattern
3.   Now add the b6th in as well
4.   Play the complete natural minor scale shape
5.   Now, find where the b5th is in relation to the pattern and add it in

Repeat this exercise at different locations on the fretboard to help you learn to mix up these different sounds.

Natural Minor Licks

Notice how the minor pentatonic scale acts as the 'backbone' for these lick examples. In most cases we're simply taking standard but effective pentatonic ideas and adding in the 2nd and/or b6th. Some picking and fingering suggestions are shown, but as always, feel free to adapt these.

(**Important**: See these licks demonstrated in **Video 7.1 Natural Minor Licks**. This is part of your **free downloadable bonus pack** - see the front of this book for details)

Lick 1 - Natural Thing

This lick is typical of how guitar players like Michael Schenker and Gary Moore use the natural minor scale. Listen to how the added notes add a slightly different flavour to what is basically a tried and tested blues-rock lick. The fingering shows you how to play it with just 3 fingers - I think this works great but you can use an alternative fingering employing all 4 fingers if you prefer.

Here's your Lick Challenge

Start by transposing this lick into the keys of D minor, C minor and G minor (in 2 octaves). This lick gives you some easy ways to work some natural minor scale into your playing - so then, use some of the ideas in this example to create at least 2 licks of your own.

Lick 2 - Nine-Up

The 2nd or 9th interval in the natural minor scale can sound great when we bend it up a semitone. You can see this happening in this example in the key of E minor (14th fret, top E string). Make sure to add this 'trick' into your soloing vocabulary.

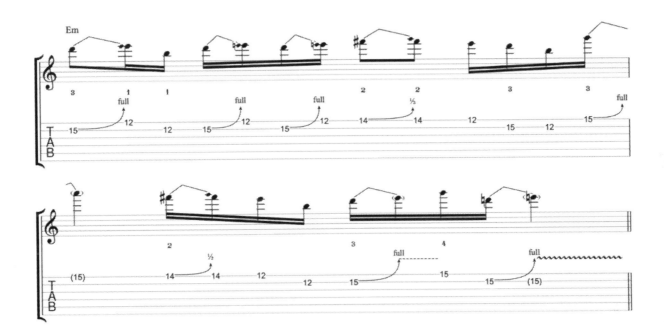

Here's your Lick Challenge

Bending the 2nd/9th up a semitone can sound great! Experiment with this idea over a backing track in the key of your choice. Explore how you can use this simple idea to modify some of your favourite pentatonic and blues scale licks, keeping a record of any useful licks you discover.

Lick 3 - Freight Train

In this example we're exploring the chunky sound of the lower notes in the scale pattern. Palm muting (notated as **P.M.**) adds a little bit of extra 'grunt' to this alternate picked idea. In the second bar you can see the 9th interval is being bent up a semitone as in the previous example, only this time it's happening on the G string (9th fret). There's a nifty fingering manoeuvre taking place in the second bar which makes the bend easier to execute - check it out, it's marked with an asterisk (*).

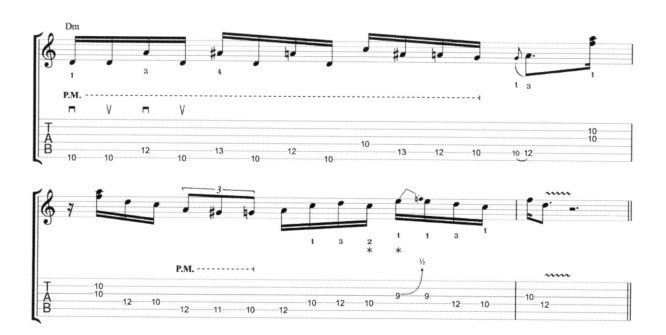

Here's your Lick Challenge

Transpose this lick into the keys of E minor, C minor A minor and G minor. Where possible, play the lick in more than one octave.

Lick 4 - Flat 'n' Furious

This example shows you some great ways to combine the natural minor scale with the dark sound of the blues scale. There are lots of useful ideas in this lick which you can sneak into your vocabulary, plus the lick is a great legato exercise. Try out the suggested fingering, it could help you get this lick really cooking!

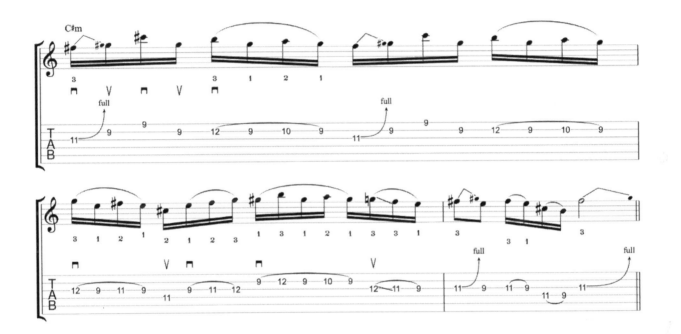

Here's your Lick Challenge

Take some of the ideas presented in the second bar of this lick. Can you use them to create some vocabulary of your own? Remember, don't be tempted to overcomplicate your ideas - search out some licks which you will actually be able to *use*.

Lick 5 - Slippin' Down

This lick kicks off with a repeating phase using the top part of the sliding G minor pentatonic pattern. In bar 2 the fun really begins, as we descend the G natural minor scale along the top strings using a combination of legato techniques. Follow the fingering for this part of the lick - it will help you play it efficiently and nail the timing, as well as building your fretting hand strength, speed and accuracy.

Here's your Lick Challenge

Use the legato ideas in bar 2 of this example to create some licks of your own. Perhaps you could try going up the scale instead of down, or make up some repeating licks? Experiment in some different keys as well.

Lick 6 - Leg-It!

Our final lick is the kind of thing a player like Paul Gilbert might play - and it's a bit of a chop-buster! We're combining legato, hammering-from-nowhere, blues scale, natural minor scale...and more. Make sure to slow this lick down, work on it in chunks, and follow the fingering and picking suggestions shown to help. Have fun!

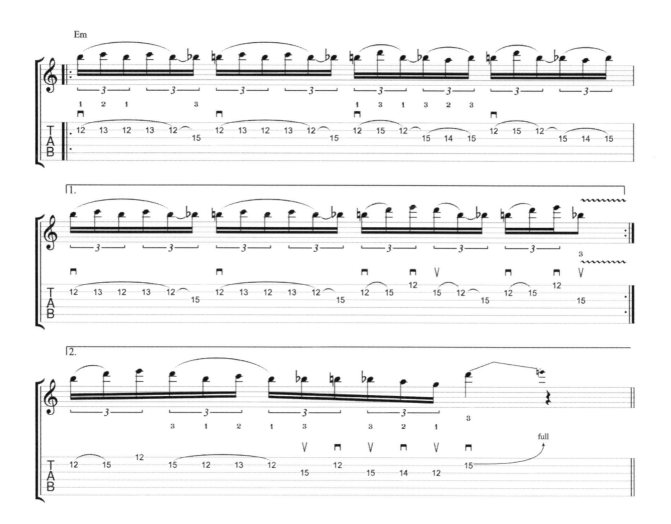

Here's your Lick Challenge

This lick uses some handy repeating lick ideas. Can you find them in the lick? Perhaps you can use them to build a few licks of your own?

The Dorian Mode

Another scale rock players use to decorate their pentatonic and blues scale ideas is the **Dorian mode**. This scale is almost identical to the natural minor scale - the only difference is that it has a **natural (unflattened) 6th** *instead* of a *b*6th. The following diagram shows the shape 1 minor pentatonic pattern with the 2nd and 6th from the Dorian mode added. I've also included the *b*5th. Compare this to the natural minor/blues scale combination from earlier so that you can see and understand the difference - all intervals are numbered to help you do this.

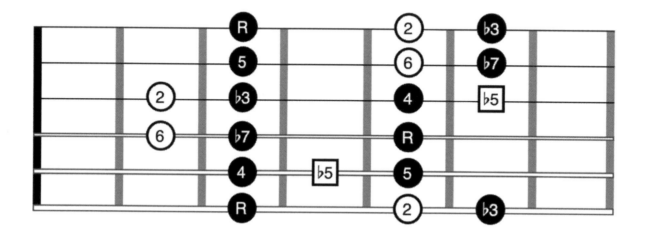

The Dorian mode is probably not used as often as the natural minor scale, but this pattern provides you with a really cool sounding selection of notes to play with, and is definitely worth exploring some time.

For detailed information on when the Dorian mode is the *perfect* scale choice, see **volume 2** and **volume 3** in my **Music Theory for Guitarists** series - for now, you can just use the following guidelines:

1.   Sometimes the *b*6th note in the natural minor scale doesn't fit with the chords you're soloing over. If this is the case then try the 6th from the Dorian mode instead - it could work better
2.   If the *b*6th and the 6th *both* sound ok over the chords, then you're free to use whichever you like (personally I prefer the natural 6th but make up your own mind)

In reality, many common rock chord progressions will work with *either*, so you can often choose which scale to use.

Dorian Licks

Most of the natural minor licks we've seen can easily be changed into Dorian licks - all we need to do is change the *b*6th to a natural 6th. The following example is a common natural minor scale idea which we've seen in this book. The *b*6th interval is highlighted with an asterisk (*).

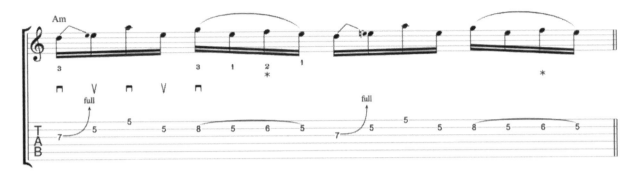

If we raise the *b*6th by a semitone it becomes the natural 6th, changing the idea into a Dorian lick. Compare the two examples, the natural 6th is now highlighted by the asterisk (*):

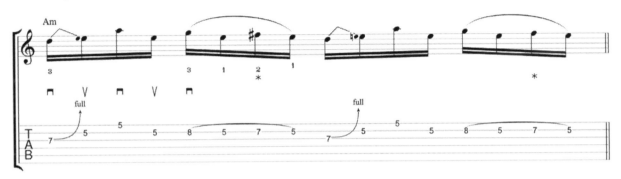

Another nice thing about the Dorian/blues scale pattern is the symmetrical fingering on the top E, B and G strings. This is shown in the following image in the key of A minor. Notice how the same frets are played on all 3 strings.

One of the best ways for you to get some Dorian ideas is to *modify* the natural minor licks from earlier in this chapter. I'll be setting you some tasks to do with this in a moment, but first let's look at a couple of short Dorian licks to help you get started. These licks combine the minor pentatonic, Dorian mode and blues scale in a variety of ways. Fingering guidelines are given in places, the picking I've left up to you.

(**Important**: See these licks demonstrated in **Video 7.2 Dorian Licks**. This is part of your **free downloadable bonus pack** - see the front of this book for details)

Lick 1 - Randy's Blues

This fun lick is a tribute to Randy Rhoads and perfectly demonstrates a few simple ways to sneak the Dorian sound into a blues lick.

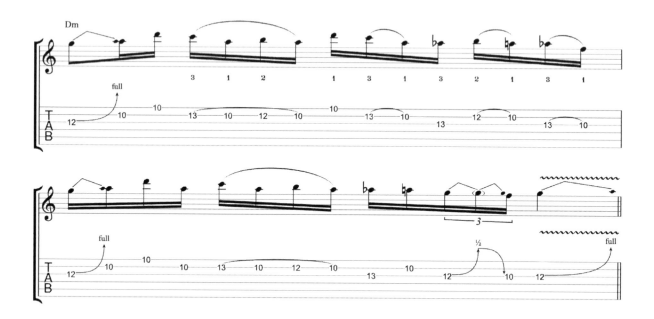

Here's your Lick Challenge

There are some useful ideas in the first bar of this example - especially on beats 2-4. Harvest these from the lick and practice them individually before combining them to create 3-4 licks of your own.

Lick 2 - Dory 'n' Dirt

The double-stop bend in bar 1 of this example is a must-know! It's bending the 6th and the 4th intervals up a semitone to the *b*7th and *b*5th to create a delicious but dirty blues sound. In bar 2 we're combining the blues scale and Dorian mode to create some tasty blues-rock ideas. Notice the semitone bend being applied to the natural 6th (11th fret, B string), this is a great Dorian bend to experiment with.

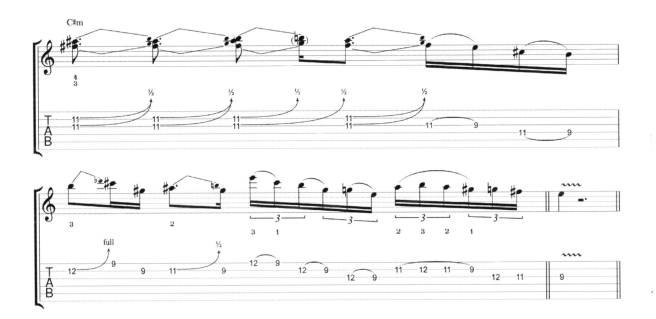

Here's your Lick Challenge

There are *lots* of useful ideas in this lick, so take some of your favourite bits and experiment. Work them into your improvisations, make up some licks which use them - just let your imagination run wild and see what you can find.

Lick 3 - Dorian Doodle

The last Dorian blues lick uses a variety of repeating ideas. Try the fingerings given for this one, they'll probably work well for you. Check out the Dorian double-stop bend at the end of this lick - doesn't it sound wicked?

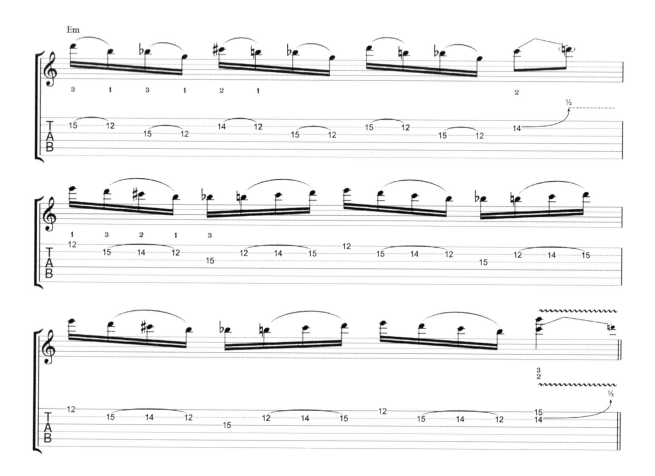

Here's your Lick Challenge

Extract the core ideas from this lick and see how you can use them in your playing. There are a range of versatile ideas which you can easily reshape into musical phrases of your own. Have fun!

Things To Do

I've shown you some really useful approaches to using the natural minor scale and the Dorian mode - but there is lots more you can discover for yourself if you enjoy the sounds these scales can give you. Some of the following exercises and tips will help point you in the right direction.

1. Convert all the natural minor licks from earlier in this chapter into Dorian licks by altering the b6th to the natural 6th. Practice switching between each version of the licks to help you easily learn to go between natural minor and Dorian soloing

2. Write out your favourite natural minor and Dorian power moves and experiment with using them. This will help you thoroughly absorb them into your playing vocabulary

3. Analyse some licks and solos by your favourite rock and metal artists. Can you spot when they are using the natural minor or Dorian modes in their playing?

4. Practice jamming over backing tracks using pentatonics with the added natural minor scale and Dorian notes. Listen and notice if they create a different flavour and mood to your solo. How would you describe these contrasting sounds?

If this lesson has whetted your appetite for the natural minor scale and Dorian mode then you might want to check out some of my other books.

See my volumes 1,2 and 3 in my **Music Theory for Guitarists** series to learn more about both of these scales and when to use them, as well as learn about other modes and scales which rock players sometimes use like the Mixolydian mode and harmonic minor scale.

My **CAGED System for Guitar** book covers the natural minor scale in much more detail too. In it you'll discover all 5 natural minor scale patterns plus lick examples from each of these. This is a great step towards mastering the natural minor scale all over the fretboard. The book also includes all the patterns for the Dorian mode (without lick examples).

That's All For This Chapter

I hope you've enjoyed this lesson covering other common rock scales. To be clear, there are *many* other scale choices as well - but I'm pretty confident that the ones we've talked about here will be the most useful to you, especially when added to your major and minor pentatonic knowledge.

So have fun experimenting with these new sounds and when you're ready we'll look at tips for putting everything together into solos which make an impact!

Ready To Move On?

- Can you convert the minor pentatonic scale into the natural minor scale by adding 2nd and *b*6th intervals?

- Have you learned the natural minor licks and 'harvested' them for soloing ideas you can use?

- Can you convert the minor pentatonic scale into the Dorian mode by adding 2nd and natural 6th intervals?

- Have you learned the Dorian licks and 'harvested' them for soloing ideas you can use?

- Have you experimented with converting the natural minor licks in this chapter into Dorian licks by altering the 6th note in the scale?

- Have you experimented with using both of these new scales in your solos and improvisations?

If the answer to these questions is yes, then when you're ready, continue to the next chapter!

Chapter 8:
Putting It Together and Building a Solo

Welcome to the final chapter in the *Rock Guitar Lick Method*. By making it this far you've demonstrated the commitment and dedication required to become a constantly improving guitar player - so kudos to you!

So far in our journey together we've looked at lots of essential rock techniques, licks, vocabulary and scales. These kinds of things are essential tools, but ultimately it's how we put all of these things *together* that really matters.

Helping you to do this is the purpose of this final chapter. We're going to look at some ideas to help you combine everything we've seen into a cohesive playing style, and create solos and improvisations which sound great *and* make musical sense to listeners. The concepts we're going to examine are some of the 'secret ingredients' you hear used by top players, but most other books and lessons *never* discuss them at all! I hope that by exposing *you* to some of these ideas on a basic level, you'll achieve your true potential as a guitar player and musician, and never run out of musical ideas and inspiration.

About This Chapter

The ideas presented in this chapter are less tangible than much of the material you've so far learned in this book. For example, instead of simply giving you a lick to learn, I may ask you to play a solo with as few notes as possible, or practice playing very soft one minute, and very loud the next.

So, be warned: some of this material may seem a bit different, or even weird at first - but my aim is to take you beyond simply playing the guitar and make you *think* about some of the elements which help to make for great music. By being aware of these elements, deliberately practicing using them, and letting them influence you - you can literally *transform* your playing over time.

Is this chapter for the beginning rock guitarist? - not really. It is aimed at someone who has already developed a good level of fluency on the guitar but who needs help in combining everything they know into a complete musical package. Having said that, a beginner *could* still benefit from being aware of some of these concepts right from the get-go. Only **you** can really decide if now is the right time to study this chapter.

Finally, you can't 'master' these concepts, they're tools which will help you to shape your guitar style throughout your entire journey as a guitarist. How you use the ideas in this chapter will change and evolve as your playing evolves, and they can be used in an in-exhaustible number of ways. With a bit of implementation, I think you'll quickly discover how powerful these concepts can be. Ok, let's get started.

Concepts for Building a Solo

I'll discuss each concept and give you some exercises to help you begin to use and understand it. In some cases I've included a short solo demonstrating the concept at work. Everything I tell you here is just a guideline, ultimately you need to decide how you like to use these ideas in your playing - there are no rights and wrongs when it comes to this stuff!

One final thing. We need to **force** ourselves to use these ideas in the practice room, in other words, we must deliberately practice using them. If we do this, they'll naturally become part of how we play. Just reading about them here will help, but we must explore them in a practical way too. I've provided you with a few ideas on how to do this in this lesson.

Repetition

One of the most powerful devices for creating musical solos is the use of **repetition**.

If a solo consists of a bunch of random licks stuck together - then it probably isn't going to make much musical sense to the person listening. Using **repetition** we can create a sense of logic and structure in our solos, and give the impression that the things we're playing are all *connected* in some way. This is nothing new, in fact, all the music you've ever heard has probably used some form of repetition - repetition of melodies, lyrics, riffs, themes etc.

Repetition can be used in *many* different ways, but let's get you started with exploring it.

Say you started a solo with one of your favourite licks. What should you play next? Well, instead of following it up with something completely *different*, maybe you could:

- Repeat the starting lick exactly the same way again
- Repeat the starting lick with a bit of variation
- Repeat the rhythm of the starting lick but change some of the notes
- Play a different lick that has a similar rhythm and 'shape'

The result: the two ideas will sound like they are **connected**, and the listener hears a logical progression from the first lick to the next - instead of hearing two completely disconnected musical ideas.

Here is a short rock solo in the key of E minor. Notice how the licks are all quite similar in some way, using the same notes and rhythms. Does the solo sound boring and repetitive, as if I've run out of licks to play?

No, I don't think so - in my opinion the repetition sounds deliberate, creating a simple solo which has structure and makes musical sense. To hear this solo watch **Video 8.1 - Repetition Demonstration.**

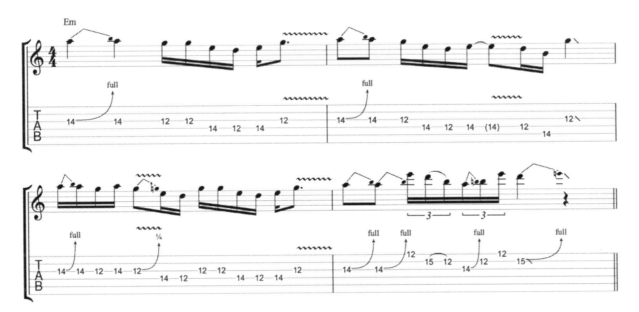

(**Note:** this solo is demonstrated over the **Minor Appetite** backing track)

Hopefully the solo study demonstrates the use of repetition in a way that is very easy to hear. Of course, make the repetition as obvious or as subtle as you like - with experience and practice you'll learn to incorporate it into your playing in whatever way feels right at the time. Notice how the solo **develops an idea** (bar 1) throughout the solo. By staying with the starting lick but recycling it into similar ideas and variations as the solo progresses, continuity and logic is created from lick to lick.

Next we'll look at an exercise to get you experimenting with using some repetition into your soloing.

Your Turn: Repetition Exercise 1

1. Choose a backing track you can solo over
2. Begin your solo with a lick of your choice
3. Leave a space
4. Repeat the lick. It can be identical, or you can vary it slightly
5. Leave a space
6. Repeat the lick again - with a variation if you choose
7. When you're ready, play a *new* lick
8. Leave a space
9. Repeat the new lick, possibly with variation
10. Continue the exercise, creating variations and introducing new licks when you want to. Make sure to leave space between each idea!

We can create some great variations on this exercise as shown in the following exercise.

Your Turn: Repetition Exercise 2

1. Choose a backing track you can solo over
2. Begin your solo with a lick of your choice
3. Leave a space
4. Follow up with a phrase which *borrows* some element(s) from the first lick. For example, you might use a recognisable chunk of the starting lick, use the same rhythm, employ the same bends/notes, or start or end your new the lick in the same way. The idea is to **link** the two ideas in some way without them being identical
5. Leave a space
6. Repeat the exercise, playing licks which are linked in some way over the backing track

Both of these simple exercises are very powerful for learning to use basic repetition because they get you really thinking about what you just played and how best to follow it up. With a bit of practice, your creative engine will start to think in this way, and you'll quickly notice that you're beginning to automatically use some repetition in your solos. After a while you'll feel like you're in much more control of what you play in your solos, instead of perhaps feeling like you're just stringing random licks together.

Are Your Solos 'Singable'?

Some of the most memorable guitar solos of all time have a 'singable' quality to them - it's possible to sing them using your voice, in the same way you might sing the words to a song. This would suggest that they feature strong and distinctive rhythmic and melodic content.

This idea is worth thinking about. Perhaps when we come to play a solo we should ask ourselves:

If I were a singer instead of a guitarist, what would I sing over this chord progression? What's the solo I'd create if I were using my voice instead of the guitar?

I've found that this can have a *profound* effect on my playing - often resulting in more melodic solos which fit the song better. It can take courage to play this way, sometimes we feel pressured to play all the 'hot licks' which we know people are impressed by - but if we can at least work *some* singable elements into our solos then it can make all the difference.

Can you think of any 'singable' guitar solos you love to hear? How can you apply what these solos teach you to your own solos?

Perhaps they:

- Use long, sustained notes for a vocal effect

- Reference the vocal melody used in the song
- Make use of simple repetitive melodies (in places)
- Make effective use of rests and space (singers need to breathe between phrases!)

Take note of how the player creates a 'singable' effect so that you can use similar techniques yourself. I'm not saying that you *always* need to play in this way - just dwell on this idea and allow it to influence you in a positive way.

Here's my attempt to demonstrate this approach over a rock ballad in the key of C# minor. I wasn't thinking of anything in particular when I created this - I was just trying to keep it as melodic and 'singable' as I could. To hear this solo watch **Video 8.2 - Singable Solo Demonstration.**

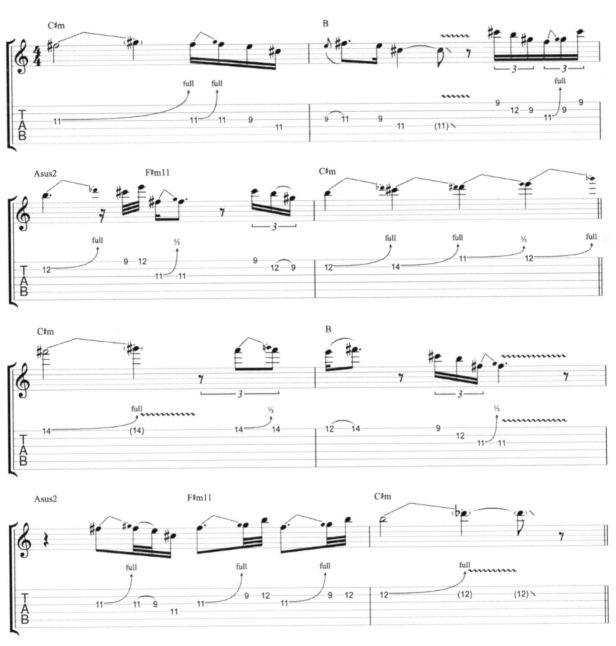

(**Note:** this solo is demonstrated over the **Classic Rock Ballad** backing track)

Your Turn: Singability Exercise

Improvise over a backing track, making your solo as singable as possible. As a tip, try not to overcomplicate things - simpler solos tend to have this quality more than 'shredding' solos do!

The idea is not necessarily to perform the *ultimate* singable solo - the point is to use this concept to *influence* your guitar style. So experiment, persevere, and *enjoy* exploring how to play more singable solos.

Strong Rhythmic Groove

Almost without exception, everything you play needs to have a strong **rhythmic groove**. This is what breathes life and character into your playing. Sloppy timing and lack of rhythmic energy will ruin even the most interesting melodic ideas. I think that a listener should be able to sense the tempo and rhythmic feel of the song *simply by listening to your solo*.

Let's try a little experiment:

- Grab your guitar and play a favourite lick or riff you know, but play it with a flat, lifeless, rhythmic feel. Toss it out, almost as if you can't be bothered to play it!
- Now, play the same thing but inject as much *rhythmic energy and vitality* into it as you can- play it as if you *really* mean business

Did you hear and feel the difference? If so, then you now know exactly what I mean by **rhythmic groove**.

Your Turn: The 'Locking In' Exercise

The first thing to practice is 'locking in' with the groove of the song. Soloing over a drum groove (and nothing else) is a great way to practice this. The lack of chords/bass etc makes it easier to focus purely on the rhythm.

1. Find a slow/medium rock drum loop (look on YouTube)
2. Choose a comfortable key and solo over the drum groove, leaving short rests between phrases
3. Really try to 'lock in' with the drums. Don't just play in-time - your licks want to be *so* synched up with the drums that they sound like they're *part* of the drum beat!
4. Remember to really **express** the rhythm of your ideas as you play them - give them rhythmic energy and vitality, like you did in the experiment from a moment ago
5. Keep going for 5-10 minutes, listening to how it sounds and tightening up the rhythm as best you can. Really try to nail that groove in your playing!

Practicing this exercise regularly will do wonders for your rhythmic groove. Of course, you can vary the drum beat to keep things from feeling stale - and because there are no chords to worry about, you can play in any key over the groove.

Rhythm is a huge topic, and there are *hundreds* of other exercises you could do to improve your rhythmic feel. Even though we're only scratching the surface here, this exercise will help you develop some of the most crucial rhythmic skills you need to master as a rock guitarist. In closing, **never neglect rhythm** in your solos - it could be even *more* important than the notes you choose to play!

Leaving Space

Think about how we naturally leave space between sentences when we talk, or how sentences, paragraphs, and headings are used in a book. Both of these things make it easier to make sense of what the speaker or writer is trying to tell us.

Leaving space in our solos has the same effect - enabling the listener to absorb our musical ideas and understand them in the context of the music. A solo which overwhelms the listener with a non-stop barrage of notes and licks, may just sound like noise to them.

Of course, there is no right or wrong *amount* of space to use in your solos - it's up to you, but learning to creatively use space is an incredibly powerful skill to attain. The key is to start thinking of space as an important *part* of your solo, not just what's left when we aren't playing anything! The exercise I'm about to show you will help you to do exactly that.

Your Turn: The Play-and- Rest Exercise

This is a really simple way to become used to using space in your solos and works a treat.

1. Choose a backing track/drum groove and a key
2. Play a phrase. It can be as long or short as you like
3. Now, force yourself to rest (stop playing!)
4. When it feels like the right time, play something
5. Now, rest again
6. Repeat like this for 5-10 minutes, making sure to include lots of 'rest'

When I started using this exercise it quickly made a *massive* difference to my playing. I'd never really thought about leaving space before then. After using the play-and-rest exercise for a while I felt like I was more in control of *what* I played and *when* I played it. It was almost like it forced me to stop playing on autopilot, and think more about the content of my solos. Leaving space started to become a part of my playing (not to say that I don't over-play sometimes!)

Some top rock players use space more than others, but at times they all use it in some way. Next time you listen to *your* favourite player, notice how he or she naturally uses space in their solos. By doing this and practicing the play-and-rest exercise, you'll naturally begin to make use of space creatively in *your* playing too.

Create Contrast

If something is the same for too long, it can become boring. We need some contrast to make things interesting - whether it's a solo, a book, a film - or even life! Contrast is a powerful tool, and worth experimenting with.

One way to think about creating contrast in your soloing is to consider things which are opposites to each other. Some possibilities could include:

- **Long** notes versus **short** notes
- **High** notes versus **low** notes
- Playing **fast** versus playing **slow**
- Playing **legato** versus playing **staccato**

You can probably think of some other devices you could use to create contrast in your solos - feel free to add them to this list.

The following study demonstrates some of these ideas being used in a short solo in the key of A minor. See if you can spot *how* I'm creating contrast in this example (answers coming in the analysis in a moment). To hear this solo watch **Video 8.3 Contrast**.

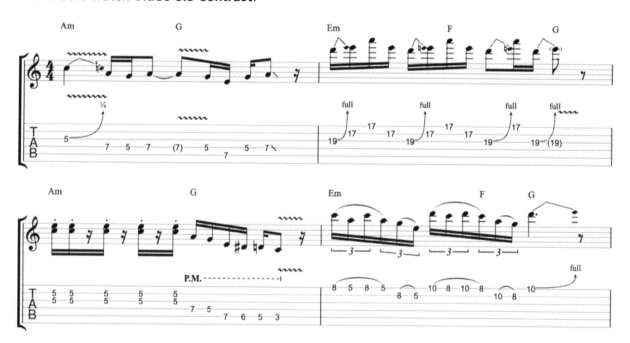

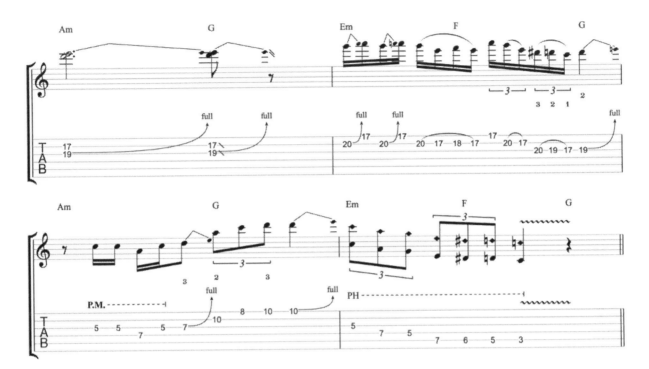

(**Note:** this solo is demonstrated over the **80's Power Pop** backing track)

In **bars 1-2** contrast is created by following a lick played low down on the neck and on the low strings with a phrase played an octave higher on the top strings (**low notes** versus **high notes**)

The staccato, palm-muted lick played in **bar 3** contrasts with the legato 'hammering from nowhere' lick in **bar 4** (**staccato** versus **legato**).

The long, sustained double-stop bend in **bar 5** is contrasted by the faster phrase in **bar 6** (**long** notes versus **short** notes).

The ascending phrase in **bar 7** is contrasted by a descending phrase in **bar 8** (**ascending** versus **descending**). Contrast is also created by the use of pinch harmonics in bar 8 to give a different effect to the sound of the notes.

Your Turn: Contrast

Explore the following ideas for creating contrast in your solo. You can do this exercise unaccompanied or use a drum loop or backing track.

1. **Long** notes versus **short** notes
2. **Slow** playing versus **fast** playing
3. **Low** notes versus **high** notes
4. Phrases which go **up** versus phrases which go **down**
5. Smooth, **legato** sounds versus 'jagged' **staccato** sounds
6. Any other ways of creating contrast you can think of

By experimenting with these approaches you're feeding your creativity all sorts of different ideas, some of which you maybe never thought about before. Over time you'll find you instinctively start to imagine and play more contrasting ideas in your solos and improvisations - making for a more interesting and distinctive guitar style.

Use Your Built-In Volume Control

Good speakers use their voice to keep an audience interested:

- They'll say some words louder than others
- They will pause for dramatic effect
- Their voice will naturally rise and fall
- The *delivery* of their speech has a built-in 'shape' to it

Without these things, their speech will sound monotone, boring - and listeners will probably tune out.

We can work this quality in our solos by being aware of *dynamic range* - put simply, the variations of volume in our playing (from soft to loud). By picking hard or soft and using techniques like slides and hammer-ons, we can become our own 'volume control' and expand the dynamic range present in our music.

Let's experiment with this now. Take any lick you know and play it as *quietly* as you can. Now, play it as *loud* as you can. Next, play it somewhere in between these two dynamic levels. Notice how this has nothing to do with how loud your amp is or what pedal you're using - it's *you* who is controlling the volume and attack. Congratulations, you just discovered your built-in volume control!

Your Turn: Dynamic Range

If you practice varying the dynamic range you use then you'll naturally start to build dynamic contrast into your solos. The following exercise is probably the simplest and most fun way to do this.

1. Improvise in a key of your choice over a backing track or drum loop
2. Start by playing a loud phrase followed by a soft phrase. Continue this step for a while
3. As the exercise becomes familiar, work in some phrases which fall somewhere between these two extremes
4. After 10-15 minutes on this exercise, just play freely with no set agenda - do you feel like there is more dynamic range in your soloing?

We could go into much more detail on this subject, but we don't need to - this simple exercise will teach you all you need to know and help you become used to using dynamic range as part of your soloing toolkit.

Economy of Ideas

Think about 'economy of ideas', and avoid throwing *everything* you can do into *every* solo you play. Doing this is the sign of a mature and musical player. Just because you are *able* to do something on the guitar, doesn't mean that you *should*!

I think our job as guitarists is to play what suits the *song*, or whatever is best for the *musical situation* we find ourselves in. Sometimes this could mean going for it with all guns blazing - other times it could mean playing nothing!

Leave Room To Build!

If you start out at maximum speed/energy level, then you've left nowhere for your solo to go to. Think about how you can leave space for your solo to build. There is no 'correct' way to do this, it's a creative thing - but some ideas you can try are:

- Starting your solo slow and gradually building up to some faster licks and phrases
- Leave more space at the start of your solo and less space as you ramp up the intensity
- Start your solo at the lower (quieter) end of the dynamic range
- Use lower notes and scale patterns to begin with, working your way up to higher frets as the solo builds

Muse on these suggestions for a while, think about how they might work. Listen to players you like - do they ever use these approaches? Then, grab your guitar and experiment with using them yourself. With a bit of work you'll find concepts like these will start to naturally influence how you sculpt your guitar solos.

Play With Conviction (and Other Assorted Wisdoms!)

Before we leave this chapter I want to share a few thoughts that I've found helpful. These might seem obvious, but I've seen them *transform* people's playing so many times that I'd be letting you down if I didn't mention them here.

These things are 'wisdoms' that I remind myself of if I'm ever feeling nervous or unsure of my playing. I've found that they've helped me a lot, I hope they help you too. Here we go...

It doesn't matter whether it's fast, slow, loud, quiet, difficult or easy - play it with conviction and never hold back

Play everything like you mean it, not as if you're trying to avoid making a mistake

Don't play timidly - play it like you believe it's worth something. People will sense this and connect with what they're hearing

Don't worry if you're not the greatest player the world has ever seen - nobody else is either! People will still enjoy listening to your playing

Mistakes are how we grow and get good - learn to enjoy making mistakes, it's how we get outside our comfort zone and progress

It's better to confidently go-for-it and screw-up than it is to hold back and achieve a bland, lifeless sense of 'perfection'

If you think about it, these are the things which really determine *how* we sound when we play - not how many scale shapes or how much theory we know! Think about these ideas, and try to relate to them in your own way, they'll make a big difference. Of course, if you have some 'wisdoms' of your own which you find help you, add them to the list.

That's All For This Chapter

I hope that this chapter has given you lots to think about as you build and develop your guitar style. As I said earlier, the concepts in this chapter can never be totally exhausted - and you'll always be able to find powerful ways to employ them no matter how good you become.

I suggest you experiment with all these concepts in the practice room. At first it may seem contrived to force yourself to employ them - it is, but this is just the first step. By practicing and thinking about these ideas, they'll naturally penetrate your creativity and your guitar style, and help you to craft everything you know into an awesome musical package.

Hopefully this chapter has given you the following benefits:

You understand how repetition, contrast, rhythmic-groove, and the other concepts examined can help you to craft better guitar solos

You've experimented with using at least some of these concepts

You're now committed to using these concepts from this point forward to help you shape everything you know into your own, unique guitar style

If this applies to you, then that's fantastic. Let's wrap everything up in the next chapter...

Congratulations!

Congratulations, you've reached the end of **The Rock Guitar Lick Method**!

Hopefully you feel like you're a completely different guitarist than you were when you first picked up this book - and that you're now equipped with what you need to play the kind of authentic rock guitar licks which your favourite guitar-heroes blast out in their solos!

I hope that I've given you a solid and practical understanding of what rock guitarists do when they play. Sure, there are *lots* of things I haven't been able to cover, but I've tried to show you what *most* rock guitarists do *most* of the time. By focusing on this, I hope to give you what you need to sound authentic, without overwhelming you with an avalanche of information and putting you off.

The method I've presented in this book is based on what I have found to work for myself and my guitar students, but we are all individuals and learn best in different ways - so feel free to modify some of my approaches to suit you. Also, supplement this book with information and ideas from other books, videos and teachers - and by listening to recordings of the great rock guitar players. There is almost *nobody* out there who you can't learn *something* from, be like a sponge and soak up as much as you can!

Finally, don't lose sight of the reason *why* we learn things like scales, licks and techniques. They are simply tools, we use them to help us be *creative*. Never forget this, and make sure that you always inject lots of experimentation, creativity and imagination into your practice sessions. This way, your playing will become an extension of who *you* are - sounds weird, but this is why the great players all sound different to each other.

I sincerely hope this book has taken your knowledge and confidence as a rock guitarist to a whole new level and given you what you need to succeed.

If you feel like it has, that's awesome!

Good luck with your playing and hope to catch up again soon in one of my other books.

Cheers!

James

Appendix 1: Rock Guitar Gear

This appendix aims to give a **simplistic** overview of the equipment rock guitarists typically use. This is a big topic, so supplement this information with your own research, there is an abundance of resources on guitar gear out there if you want to know more.

Tips for Choosing a Guitar

- Most rock guitarists choose a solid body electric guitar (i.e. the body is a solid block of wood not partially hollow). This gives the heavy, biting sound associated with rock and metal
- What type of guitar does your favourite player use? This may help you to narrow it down when faced with an overwhelming number of models to choose from
- If the guitar you want costs megabucks, then don't worry - you can normally find something very similar in lower price brackets. Some of the lower priced guitars these days are amazing. When it comes to guitars, you don't *always* get what you pay for!
- The sound of a guitar is highly influenced by *how* you play it, and your guitar will sound better and better as your playing improves

Pickups

The type of **pickups** a guitar uses is probably overall more important than the look and brand. The two main types of pickup are **single coils** and **humbuckers** (do a quick internet search if you're not familiar with how they look).

- In general, humbuckers have a heavier, chunkier sound. Single coils give you a thinner, brighter sound
- Both pickup types can work well for playing rock, but the heavier sound of humbuckers is a very popular choice. I suggest trying a few guitars fitted with both types to hear the difference
- A guitar with 2 or 3 pickups will give you a larger range of sounds than a guitar with just one pickup
- In general, most rock players use the bridge pickup (nearest the bridge of the guitar) most of the time. This gives the tight, punchy sound heard on most rock recordings

Strings

- Most players use either a set of 9-42 gauge strings (light and easier to bend) or 10-46 gauge strings (slightly fatter sound, a little harder to bend). There are other choices, but both of these options are a good starting point
- When it comes to strings you do normally get what you pay for - super-cheap strings tend to sound cheap and not last very long

Amps and Pedals

The amplifier you plug into has a *huge* impact on the sound you get. Let's look at some basic considerations when choosing an amp.

- Choose an amp which is built for playing rock and can give you an overdriven or distorted sound
- Most of the classic rock sounds come from tube or valve amps. Many rock guitarists still use these, but there are some great digital amps which will give you the sound of a valve amp, and often for a much smaller price tag
- If you have an amp which *doesn't* have built in distortion then you will want to get a **distortion pedal**. Basically you plug your guitar into the pedal, then plug the pedal into the amp. The controls on the pedal are then used to shape the distorted sound. There are thousands of distortion pedals out there, and you'll easily find one you like the sound of
- You may not need an amp at all. There are many **software applications** which will give you a similar sound. Connect your guitar to your phone or tablet using the appropriate hardware, and you're good-to-go

Setting the Amp

There is no 'right' amp setting because amp designs vary so much. I can make a few suggestions, but to be clear, these are a **simplified guideline** only - adapt them to suit your amp.

- The manual for your amp may contain suggested settings to get you started
- The **equalisation** (eq) section of an amp controls how bassy/ bright your sound is. I normally set my **bass** and **treble** dials to **6-7**. The **mid** dial I set to around **4**. You'll need to experiment with these settings - some amps don't even have a middle control!
- The **gain** knob on an amp controls the amount of distortion. I set it at **6 - 10** depending on how much distortion I want. The gain is sometimes labelled something different (e.g. drive, overdrive)
- The **volume** or **master volume** control on the amp controls the overall loudness level - set this to where you (and your neighbours) like it
- You may have other controls on your amp like reverb, presence or boost - experiment with these to find where you like them set to

Hopefully you've got some helpful ideas from this information. Obviously, I've only covered the bare minimum - and there is certainly not a shortage of websites and blogs which deal with this topic if you want to know more. Remember too, you don't need the perfect sound and setup *right now*, it's just about getting something which is good enough - many of the greatest players started with very humble gear!

Appendix 2:
Rhythmic Reading Basics

Being able to read simple rhythmic notation is a useful skill for any musician, and it's not difficult to do once you understand some of the basics. So let's take a crash-course in rhythm reading right now.

Most rock music is in 'four-four' time. This simply means that there are 4 beats in each bar of music - we're feeling/counting the passing beats in groups of four. This is why people normally count in a band '*one, two, three, four*' - they're showing the musicians where the beats are and how fast they are passing by.

Sometimes you'll see a **time signature** written at the start of the *stave* (the system of 5 lines which we write music notation on). The four-four time signature is highlighted by the arrow in the following image.

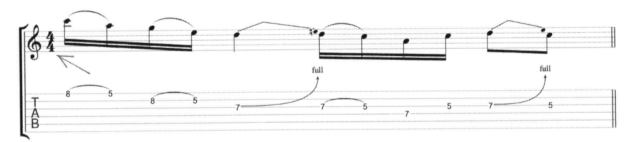

There are other time signatures too, for example 3/4, 6/8 and 5/4 - but rock music is nearly always in four-four time.

Note Values

A note's *value* tells us how long it sounds for, with a long note having a larger value than a short note. You can tell the value of a note from how it *looks* - its shape, whether it has a tail etc. Let's look at the common note values and see what they look like written down. If you're wondering how we play them and what they sound like, that's coming very soon.

Quarter Notes, Eighth Notes and Sixteenth Notes

The following image shows a **quarter note (¼ note)**. A quarter note has a value of **1 beat**. So if you played a quarter note on your guitar it would sound for 1 beat.

quarter note (value = 1 beat)

The next image shows **eighth notes (8th notes)**. An eighth note has a value of **half a beat**, so if you played a series of eighth notes, each one would last for half a beat. Multiple eighth notes are often joined up or *beamed* together to make them easier to read. You can see this in the second bar of the following image.

eighth notes or 8th notes (value = half a beat)

The next image shows **sixteenth notes (16th notes)**. These each have a value of a **quarter of a beat**. So if you played a series of sixteenth notes, each one would last for one quarter of a beat. Multiple sixteenth notes are normally *beamed* together to make them easier to read as shown in the second bar.

sixteenth or 16th notes (value = quarter of a beat)

You can also think of these note values as **subdivisions** or **fraction**s of the beat. A quarter note is a full beat. Split the beat into 2 equal parts and we get 8th notes, split it into 4 equal parts and we get 16th notes. Hopefully this is making sense. If you're a bit confused, keep going - things will probably make more sense once you start playing some of these rhythms.

Reading and Playing Rhythms

One of the easiest ways to get used to reading rhythms is to count them out loud as you play them on an open string. We'll do this now using the open top E string on the guitar.

Start by counting out a slow even beat - *one, two, three, four, one, two, three, four* etc.

Play the open top string along with the count, once on each beat. Continue the counting as you play the note. When you do this you're playing **quarter notes**. The following example should help clarify this. The count is shown above the stave and tab is included to help. The beat is marked with an asterisk (*) to help you see how the notes and the beat line up.

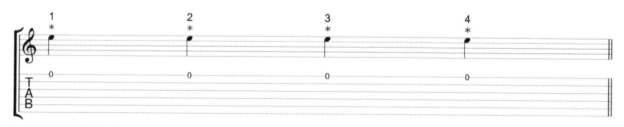

Now play the open top string **twice** on each beat. Count this as '1 &, 2 &, 3 &, 4 &'. Now you're playing **eighth notes**. In the following example the vocal count is shown above the stave and the beat is marked with an asterisk (*) to help you keep your place. Practice this for a while until it feels natural.

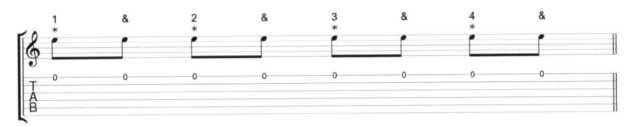

Now play the open top string **four times** on each beat. Count this as '1 a & a, 2 a & a, 3 a & a, 4 a & a'. Now you're playing **sixteenth notes**. In the following example the vocal count is shown and the beat is marked with an asterisk (*) to help. Practice playing and counting sixteenth notes until it feels comfortable.

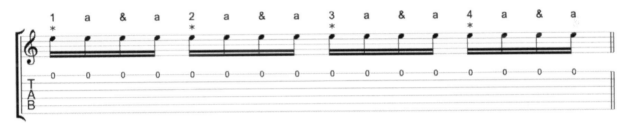

Of course, rhythmic values are frequently mixed up. If they weren't then music would get pretty boring, all the notes would be the same length.

Rhythm reading skills can help you to work out the rhythm of an example without having to listen to it dozens of times, really speeding up the learning process. Imagine you wanted to learn the following simple lick:

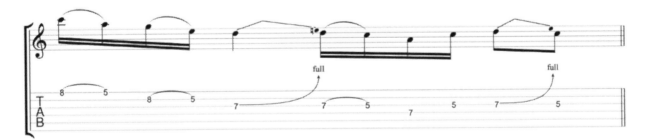

You could start by slowly counting through the rhythm using the methods I've described:

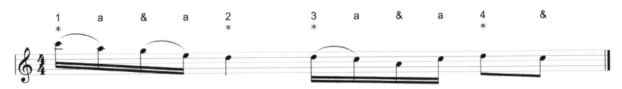

Then, use the tab to add the notes to the rhythm. The added elements like bends and pull-offs make this example appear a bit different. Don't let this throw you - you can still clearly see the rhythm written on the top stave:

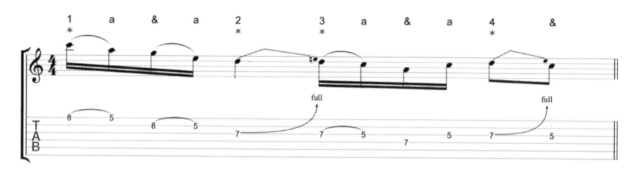

If you persevere with this process as you work through this book then you'll soon become comfortable reading simple rhythms - a very useful skill to acquire.

Triplets and Sextuplets

We can group the note values seen so far into groups of three to get **triplet** rhythms. These are extremely common in virtually all music. Let's look at the most common triplet rhythms you'll see.

If we condense three equally spaced 8th notes into a single beat we get **eighth note triplets**. These are shown in the following image.

These can be counted '1 & a, 2 & a, 3 & a, 4 & a'. You can also think of a triplet as sounding like the word 'widdly'. This may sound silly, but a rhythmic word like this can help us to learn the sound of common rhythms, and in some cultures this is how rhythm is learned. The following exercise shows both of these approaches. Practice them both to learn the common sound of 8th note triplets. The beat is marked with an asterisk (*) to help you keep your place.

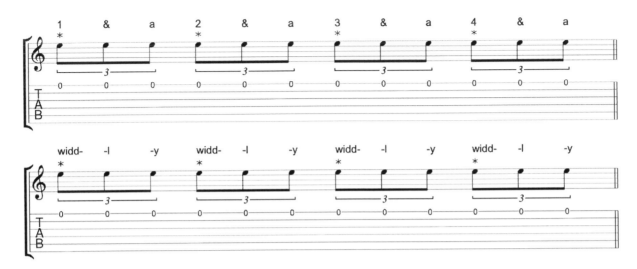

Sextuplets or **16th note triplets** are when we condense two triplets into a single beat. They basically sound like 8th note triplets played twice as fast. The following image shows you what these look like - notice how the beat is now divided into six equal parts.

The following exercise shows how you can count sextuplets - really just a variation on how we counted triplets. Try playing these on your guitar, slowing it down as much as necessary to fit the six notes into each beat.

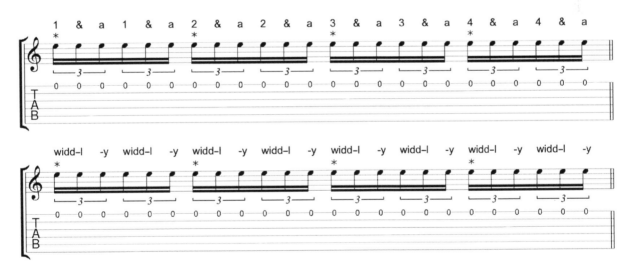

And that's your crash-course in rhythm reading. I've tried to condense lots of useful knowledge into a short lesson, and you may need to read through everything again to make it super-clear. Of course, we could go much deeper into this topic, but I'm guessing rhythm reading is not the reason you bought this book! My aim is just to give you a basic introduction, if you want to develop this skill further then there are many resources to help you do this.

More Guitar Books by James Shipway

Music Theory for Guitarists, the Complete Method Book, Volumes 1, 2 & 3

The CAGED System for Guitar

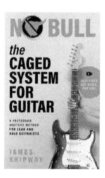

Barre Chords for Guitar

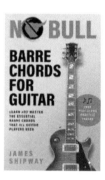

Music Theory for Guitarists, Volume 1

Music Theory for Guitarists, Volume 2

Music Theory for Guitarists, Volume 3

Circle of Fifths for Guitar

Blues Soloing for Guitar, Volume 1

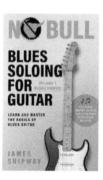

Blues Soloing for Guitar, Volume 2

*If you've enjoyed this book, you might want to check out some of the other books I've written, as shown on the previous page. To find out more about each one, scan the QR code shown here, or visit Headstock Books at **headstockbooks.com***

Most titles are available as paperbacks, ebooks and hardcovers from Amazon, Apple, Google Play, Kobo, Barnes & Noble, and by request from your local library or book shop.

Check Out My *Total Guitar Lab* Online School

Want to study specific guitar styles and topics with me as your guitar teacher? Well you can, with my online guitar community **Total Guitar Lab**! Join and get instant access to *all* my premium guitar courses *plus* live training, workshops and Q&A sessions. Learn more and discover the amazing results guitarists have been getting with my training. Visit **totalguitarlab.com**

Single Courses Also Available:

Some of my guitar courses are available as stand-alone products. This means they are yours to keep and go through at your own pace as many times as you like. Courses are made up of step-by-step video lessons, downloadable backing tracks, audio lessons and detailed tab workbooks complete with homework tasks and checklists to make sure you reach your goals.

The following courses are currently available. You can find them at **totalguitarlab.com** :

Blues Guitar Launchpad

The perfect course for the beginner to intermediate electric blues guitarist. Learn all the essential blues scales, how to play the 12 bar blues, authentic blues licks, string bending and vibrato techniques plus complete solo studies in the styles of blues legends like Eric Clapton, Stevie Ray Vaughan, Freddie King, Otis Rush and others! Learn more at: **totalguitarlab.com**

Minor Pentatonic Mastery

Perfect for the more experienced rock or blues player who wants to conquer the minor pentatonic scale all over the guitar neck! *Minor Pentatonic Mastery* takes you step-by-step through all the ways to play the minor pentatonic scale on the guitar. Learn all 5 'box patterns' and how to use them to play killer blues and rock licks, discover 'sliding' scale patterns, the 'Rule of 2' to use for connecting it all up and loads more powerful soloing and improvising tips to use in building an awesome pentatonic soloing vocabulary. Learn more at: **totalguitarlab.com**

Rock Guitar Lick Lab

Aimed at the intermediate rock guitar player who wants to explode their playing with the licks and techniques used by the biggest names in rock and metal guitar. Discover essential rock bending licks, repeating licks, alternate picked licks, extended blues scale licks and stretch and sequence licks and how to use them in your playing for explosive rock and metal guitar solos!

You'll also learn essential technique tips to get the licks sounding great and how to use everything in the course to easily start generating killer rock licks of your own. Learn more at: **totalguitarlab.com**

'Stormy Monday' Blues Workshop

A two hour workshop showing you everything you need to master and enjoy this classic blues song. You'll start by learning the Stormy Monday chord progression and the sliding riffs used in all the classic versions of the song. Then discover how to solo over Stormy Monday using blues scale, major pentatonic, BB Box and more. Includes two complete solo studies, a tab workbook and backing tracks. Learn more at: **totalguitarlab.com**

Solo Blues Jamming Workshop

Learn a step-by-step method for combining chords and licks into your very own solo blues jams! Includes play-a-long tracks, drill videos and more to help you master this fun way of playing blues guitar. Learn more at: **totalguitarlab.com**

Notebuster

Want to learn all the notes on the fretboard in the quickest and most pain free way possible? **Notebuster** will show you how! After this short mini course, you'll be able to find *any* note on *any* string *...anywhere* on the guitar. Learn more at: **totalguitarlab.com**

Follow me on YouTube:

Search for James Shipway Guitar on YouTube and subscribe for hours of free video lessons!

Rock Lick Method for Guitar
by James Shipway

Published by Headstock Books
headstockbooks.com

Copyright © James Shipway 2023

All rights reserved. This book or parts thereof may not be reproduced in any form, stored in any retrieval system, or transmitted in any form by any means - electronic, mechanical, photocopy, recording, or otherwise - without prior written permission of the publisher, except as provided by the United Kingdom copyright law. For permission requests, contact: info@headstockbooks.com

Paperback ISBN: 978-1-914453-16-8
Hardcover ISBN: 978-1-914453-17-5 / 978-1-914453-18-2
Ebook ISBN: 978-1-914453-15-1

Made in the USA
Middletown, DE
10 September 2023

38304223R00093